MINORITY REPORT

UNPOPULAR THOUGHTS ON EVERYTHING
FROM ANCIENT CHRISTIANITY
TO ZEN-CALVINISM

MINORITY REPORT

UNPOPULAR THOUGHTS ON EVERYTHING
FROM ANCIENT CHRISTIANITY
TO ZEN-CALVINISM

CARL R TRUEMAN

MENTOR

ISBN 1-84550-317-1
ISBN 978-1-84550-317-8

© Carl R. Trueman

10 9 8 7 6 5 4 3 2 1

Published in 2008
in the
Mentor Imprint
by
Christian Focus Publications,
Geanies House, Fearn, Ross-shire,
IV20 1TW, Scotland, UK

www.christianfocus.com

Cover design by Alister MacInnes

Printed and bound by CPD, Wales

CONTENTS

For John and Peter

INTRODUCTION

The following collection of writings is presented as a companion volume to my earlier book for Christian Focus Publications, *The Wages of Spin*. It is a companion in the sense that, just as a member of Christian Focus's management team described the earlier volume as a book without a theme and with no obvious market, so this fulfills the same nightmare criteria for the marketing department.

Flippancy aside, this collection does represent a continuation of the project I started in the first book: it is a collection of essays and shorter writings, drawn mainly from my monthly *Wages of Spin* column for the e-zine, Reformation 21 (www. reformation21.org), whose overall agenda is to provoke the readers to think more critically about their faith and the world around them. My purpose is, first and foremost, to make people sit up and think; whether they agree or disagree with me is of only secondary importance. I also hope that they demonstrate that the old orthodoxies of the Christian faith do not need to be stuffy, pompous, out-of-date, or allied to a dusty, unattractive, and cadaverous piety.

The first part of the book consists of four longer essays which perhaps require some comment by way of introduction in order to set them in context. Chapter One is a revised version of my inaugural lecture as Professor of Historical Theology and Church History at Westminster Theological Seminary, Pennsylvania in 2005. By the very nature of the genre it is a broad manifesto for the practice of the discipline of church history within a seminary setting. In setting out my philosophical and methodological agenda for church history at Westminster, I focus on the faulty historiography underlying some post-conservative approaches to the Reformed tradition, not because I do not think that the kind of questions being asked by some post-conservatives are not important but because I believe that accurate historical understanding of the Christian tradition is essential for a truly critical approach to the present, and a fruitful articulation of the faith once for all delivered in the contemporary context.

Chapter Two first appeared in *Themelios*, the evangelical theological journal which I edited from 1998 to 2007. In it I draw together the thoughts of two men who both died in 2003: Carl Henry, the American evangelical leader and thinker, and Edward Said, the Palestinian intellectual, literary critic, and political activist. I had profited from them both: as a young Christian, Henry's writings had offered me a model of thoughtful evangelical writing; then, I had developed a love for Said's work both because we shared a mutual passion for the novels of Joseph Conrad, an interest in the political readings of literary texts, and an appreciation for the better aspects of postmodern critical theory as well as a deep suspicion of the disempowering impact that postmodernism, at its most arcane and trivial, could have.

Chapter Three is published here for the first time. In late 2006, I found myself embroiled in an internet debate about the undeniable Holocaust Denial of the perplexingly popular (in some circles) Rousas J. Rushdoony, with some of his more distasteful followers. At about the same time, I was invited by the Veritas Forum at Bryn Mawr College to deliver a lecture in the spring of 2007. Hannah Arendt's study of Adolf Eichmann, a classic of twentieth-century journalism and cultural analysis, seemed the obvious choice. The lecture went as well as anything I have ever done; but the discussion afterwards was a disaster. I was badly beaten up (intellectually speaking) by a self-described "secular postmodern Jewish philosopher." He proved a very different and far more formidable opponent than the various middle-aged evangelical faux-postmodernists of the kind whose theology so often seems little more than an attempt to cope with their midlife crises and generational disconnect with youth culture. The Bryn Mawr experience was sobering and humbling, far less pleasant but far more instructive than mere preaching to the gallery; and, as Nietzsche says, "That which does not destroy me makes me stronger." It was also a salutary lesson that apologetics is about more than demonstrating the inconsistent presuppositions of an opponent's position; my opponent that night did not care about such. Refuting a book or an abstract idea is one thing; refuting a flesh-and-blood opponent is quite another.

Chapter Four was a tough piece to write. It is a critical review of *Is the Reformation Over?*, a book by Mark Noll and Carolyn Nystrom. I have been the recipient of numerous acts of personal kindness and encouragement from Mark Noll over the years, and to criticize with respect and charity someone who is such a well-respected and distinguished figure, as well as one for whom I have great affection and respect, is no easy task. A letter from Mark in response to the review indicated that he neither took offense at what I said, nor was persuaded by it! Yet I continue to believe that the Reformation is **not** over and that we lose central elements of the gospel and of the Christian life if we think that it is.

The pieces in Part Two are all shorter and speak for themselves. They deal with themes as disparate as the purpose of history, blogging, pop culture, psalm singing, *American Idol*, ancient church "holy man" narratives, and Zen-Calvinism. I hope that they offer models of what a critical approach to Christianity and culture might look like and help the reader to think more deeply about these and other issues. As with *The Wages of Spin*, I end with an attempt at pastiche, this time of a Sherlock Holmes story, which first appeared in *Themelios*.

As always, it is necessary to thank all those who have helped to make the book possible. At Christian Focus, Willie Mackenzie helped to see the project through from beginning to end, with limitless patience, good humor, and near total disbelief when I finally submitted the manuscript.

Others to thank include Derek Thomas and Jeremy Smith at Reformation 21. I am, at the time of writing, the most complained-about contributor to the e-zine and am most grateful to both of these gentlemen for encouragement and for filtering the nastier correspondence. Christians do write the most spectacularly humorless hatemail; what motivates people to waste their time in this way is a mystery to me, but such letters and e-mails do perversely encourage me to continue rattling cages; and they also provide some of the best satirical material for the likes of Rodney Trotter, Tony "the Gent" Pinnochio, the Rev. Sanc T. Monious, and my other friends on the Ref21 blog. Thankfully, there are also those who take a more positive view of my writing and I am extremely grateful to those more generous-spirited readers who have taken the time to write to encourage me over the years, and who have also stimulated my thinking on numerous matters through their thoughtful comments and questions. Such kind notes are worth more than gold.

Thanks are also due to various other people for less direct help. To Ligon Duncan and C. J. Mahaney for constant prayerful support, kind words, and sound wisdom. To Dave Strain and Paul Levy for their fellowship in the Lord and their entertaining hospitality whenever I pass through London. To Sandy Finlayson for keeping me sane (relatively speaking) at Westminster Theological Seminary. To Bill Edgar for constantly encouraging me to write. To Hunter Powell, my star Westminster student, now a PhD candidate at the University of Cambridge, for his enthusiastic encouragement over the last few years. To Jen Troutman and Martha Dunson for running Academic Affairs so efficiently that the Dean still had time to write. To Pete Lillback and Dick Dabney for solid support and friendship during interesting times at the Seminary.

And, of course, my greatest debt, humanly speaking, is to my wife, Catriona, for her love and constant friendship. Finally, I must not forget my two sons, John and Peter. At last dad's managed to dedicate a book to you.

PART ONE

Part One

RAGE, RAGE AGAINST THE DYING OF THE LIGHT[1]

INTRODUCTION

Having been unable to find a suitable quotation from Bob Dylan as a title for my inaugural lecture, I have chosen instead a line from a famous poem by his partial namesake, Dylan Thomas. The whole stanza reads as follows:

Do not go gentle into that good night,
Old age should burn and rave at close of day;
Rage, rage against the dying of the light.

My reason for choosing as my opening shot Dylan Thomas's rant against the passive resignation of old age in the face of death is simply this: today, both old age and church history are generally regarded as irrelevant. In a culture obsessed with youth and driven by consumption, old age is something of an embarrassment. It is an unproductive, unmarketable concept; and, in a church which so often apes the larger culture, church

---

[1] This is a revision of Carl R. Trueman's inaugural lecture as Professor of Historical Theology and Church History at Westminster Theological Seminary on November 16, 2005.

history is usually regarded as having little or nothing of use to say. My purpose, therefore, is to cast a critical eye on this assumption, and to indicate that Westminster Seminary church historians are not simply going to acquiesce in the consensus concerning their irrelevance, but that they fully intend to rage, rage against the dying of the historical light.[2]

A variety of factors contribute to the anti-historical thrust of the modern age, as I have argued elsewhere.[3] Suffice it to say today, however, that I believe that in a society dominated by ideologies of novelty and innovation—ideologies driven by the agendas of science, of capital, and of consumerism—the past will always be cast in terms which put it at a disadvantage in relation to present and future. In fact, it is vitally necessary in such societies for the past to be inferior; this is one important means of validating the present and justifying the future. Dare one say it, in America, a nation built on notions of an expanding frontier and of manifest destiny, a nation whose self-actualization is always seen as being just over the next horizon, such present-future orientation is particularly strong. But it is not just in America that such a viewpoint exerts its grip; it is a Western phenomenon as a whole, with even our language indicating this underlying value scheme: *innovative, original, ground-breaking* have, on the whole, positive connotations; *traditional, conservative, old-fashioned* have, on the contrary, negative ones. Within such a cultural framework, can history really serve any function other than that of a traveling freak show which parades the grotesques, the monsters, and the mediocrities of the past in order to allow the modern world to feel good about itself and its future?

---

[2] It is worth noting that Westminster embodies this counter-cultural trend in the emphasis it gives to church history in the curriculum, with full courses being taught on Ancient Church, Medieval Church, The Reformation, and Modern Age. Most seminaries now compress church history into two courses, covering early church to medieval, and then Reformation to modern.

[3] See "Reckoning with the Past in an Anti-Historical Age" in Carl R. Trueman, *The Wages of Spin* (Fearn: Christian Focus, 2004), 15–38.

A further problem for history as a discipline is the cluster of philosophies which are bracketed together under the general term *postmodernism*. Postmodernism has allegedly rendered implausible the whole idea of grand narratives and of the accessibility of truth in any traditional way. In a world of no grand narratives, of course, there can be no history in any referential sense, only various incommensurable narratives by which historians express their own values and tastes. Writing history is thus swallowed up in the politics of the present. Postmoderns tells us that because of this radically relativizing insight we therefore live an age of epochal change, where everything once certain is now exposed as negotiable and volatile, and that a fundamental cultural paradigm shift has occurred.[4]

As a historian, of course, I am never impressed by claims about epochal events and paradigm shifts. I am too well aware that every age has made claims to being epochal; the great Bob Dylan may well have sung, "Oh my name it is nothin', my age it means less," but nobody has ever really believed such sentiments about themselves and their own time. On the contrary, human beings have consistently and continuously engaged in the creative struggle to transform culture and to leave their mark on the world around them. This surely indicates something about the amazing and awesome human drive to make a difference, to make my name and my age the decisive one. Is the postmodern turn of epochal significance? Only time will really tell, but if I were a betting man, I would wager heavily against it being so.

At a more sophisticated level, my skepticism about postmodernism is rooted in my attraction to the arguments of

---

[4] A good grasp of the epistemological impact of postmodernism on the practice of history can be gained from reading Alun Munslow, *Deconstructing History* (London: Routledge, 2006). This is the second edition of a book which is now a standard text in deconstructionist approaches to history. A useful analysis, and thoughtful, moderate response, to postmodern historical method is Joyce Appleby, Lynn Hunt, and Margaret Jacob, *Telling the Truth about History* (New York: W. W. Norton, 1995).

critical theorists like Frederic Jameson, Perry Anderson, and Terry Eagleton.[5] They argue that postmodernism, with all of its vibrantly creative, chaotic, challenging, and exciting insights, is actually the cultural logic of late capitalism, to use Jameson's phrase. I myself prefer to speak of the cultural logic of *advanced consumerism* so as to avoid the prescriptive political and eschatological implications of Jameson's Marxism, but his basic point is, I believe, sound. To defend this thesis would take too much time today, so a single quotation from Karl Marx himself will have to suffice. In the *Communist Manifesto* Marx describes with unnerving foresight the epistemological and ethical anarchy which modernity, extended to its very limits, globalized and universalized, will bring with it:

> The bourgeoisie has stripped of its halo every occupation hitherto honoured and looked up to with reverent awe... Constant revolutionizing of production, uninterrupted disturbance of all social conditions, everlasting uncertainty and agitation distinguish the bourgeois epoch from all earlier ones. All fixed, fast-frozen relations, with their train of ancient and venerable prejudices and opinions, are swept away, all new-formed ones become antiquated before they can ossify. All that is solid melts into air, all that is holy is profaned, and man is at last compelled to face with sober senses, his real conditions of life, and his relations with his kind.[6]

---

[5] Among Frederic Jameson's voluminous critical works, see especially *Postmodernism, or, The Cultural Logic of Late Capitalism* (Durham: Duke University Press, 1991); idem, *A Singular Modernity: Essay on the Ontology of the Present* (London: Verso, 2002). Perry Anderson's basic thesis on postmodernity is detailed in *The Origins of Postmodernity* (London: Verso, 1998). Terry Eagleton's work possesses that unique combination for someone writing on postmodernism of being witty, incisive, and comprehensible: see his *The Illusions of Postmodernism* (Oxford: Blackwell, 1996); idem, *After Theory* (New York: Basic Books, 2004). Many of the essays in *The English Novel* (Oxford: Balckwell, 2004) also demonstrate lines of critique regarding many of the metanarratival claims made by postmodern thinkers.

[6] From "The Communist Manifesto," in Karl Marx, *The Revolutions of 1848: Political Writings I* (London: Penguin, 1973).

All that is holy is profaned: pardon the pun, but full marks to Marx for here predicting precisely the kind of anarchic world which would produce both the highly sophisticated philosophical hedonism of Michel Foucault and the crass redneck shenanigans of the Jerry Springer Show.

If, of course, postmodernism, with all of its disdain for history in any traditional sense, is the ideology of advanced consumerism, then it can just as easily be described as the quintessential ideology of modern America; indeed, in modern America, and in the West which follows America's social and economic lead, it is surely interesting to note that just about anything can be believed, however absurd, and any moral precedent can be overturned, however well-established, provided that such action can be successfully marketed as enhancing the American consumerist dream. Whether it is the nature of human sexuality, the definition of marriage, or access to abortion and euthanasia, American public morality is increasingly that of the marketplace, and moral truth is that which the cultural market forces permit, or, in some cases, demand. Think, for example, of the recent emergence of phenomena such as gay tourism and gay television channels. Would these things happen if they did not present opportunities for moneymaking? And can one overestimate how these things themselves then feed into and reinforce the social normalization of homosexuality as a lifestyle *choice* (and I use the word *choice* precisely to make the point about the connection with the consumer mentality).[7]

---

[7] Of course, I assume here that the dynamic or logic of the marketplace is itself complex and not something which is simply driven either by supply or by demand. Rather, there is a complex negotiation between supplier and consumer which also takes into account wider cultural factors, such as previous history, established values, etc. Thus, for example, programs like *Will and Grace* and *Friends* in the USA or *Eastenders* in the UK, which have undoubtedly done much not simply to reflect but also to shape wider cultural understandings of sexual morality, relationship, etc, have not simply done so by presenting an alternative reality which the public has then absorbed in some uncritical manner; other factors, such as the rise in disposable income,

This is where my narrative today connects to evangelicalism. If postmodernism was always destined to be the cultural logic of modern America, with its consumer driven economy and cultural mores, then it was arguably inevitable that it was also destined to be the ideology of evangelicalism, which, with its individualism, its pragmatism, and its functional disdain for history, is Americanized religion par excellence.[8]

Now, there has been much hoo-hah over recent years about how the church in general, and evangelicalism in particular, must embrace many aspects of the (nebulous) cultural conditions called postmodernism.[9] In part, this is built upon a historiography which I shall presently call into serious question. First, however, I want to draw attention to the fact that the proponents of postmodern or post-conservative evangelicalism generally consider themselves to be saying something new. They are calling, as they see it, for a fundamental recasting or revisioning of evangelical theology in postmodern, anti-Enlightenment categories. At this point, I want to begin to demonstrate the value of history as a *critical* discipline by applying to postmodern evangelicalism

the material limits and possibilities of professional urban life, the wider significance of the televisual media in general, along with many other factors, have all played their part. Yet I believe my central point is sound: the marketplace is perhaps the single most powerful nexus of cultural forces in the modern Western world.

[8] The one possible rival to this characterization of evangelicalism as *the* quintessential American religion is Mormonism: see Nathan Hatch, *The Democratization of American Christianity* (New Haven: Yale University Press, 1989). For a thorough critique of the impact of consumerism and American values on evangelical Protestantism in the USA, see the tetralogy by David Well, *No Place for Truth* (Grand Rapids: Eerdmans, 1993), *God in the Wasteland* (Grand Rapids: Eerdmans, 1994), *Losing Our Virtue* (Grand Rapids: Eerdmans, 1998), and *Above all Earthly Pow'rs* (Grand Rapids: Eerdmans, 2005).

[9] See, for example, Stanley J. Grenz, *A Primer on Postmodernism* (Grand Rapids: Eerdmans, 1996), esp. 161–74; Stanley J. Grenz and John R. Franke, *Beyond Foundationalism: Shaping Theology in a Postmodern Context* (Louisville: Westminster John Knox Press, 2001); also John R. Franke, "Reforming Theology: Toward a Postmodern Reformed Dogmatics," in *Westminster Theological Journal* 65 (2003), 1–26.

the principle articulated so well by Quentin Skinner, the Cambridge historian and philosopher: when reading an historical text, Skinner points out, one must not simply ask what the writer of the text is *saying*; one must also, and more importantly, ask what the writer of the text is *doing*.[10]

Now, when one approaches the major texts of postmodern evangelicalism and asks what they are saying, the answer is exciting: they claim they are opening up radical new directions for theology; but when one approaches the same texts and asks what they are *doing*, the answer is somewhat more prosaic. Far from pointing to new ways of doing theology, these texts are on the whole appropriating an admittedly new idiom, that of postmodernism, in order to accomplish a very traditional and time-honored task: they are articulating a doctrinally minimal, anti-metaphysical "mere Christianity." Like pouting teenagers in pre-torn designer jeans and Che Guevara tee-shirts, they look angry and radical but are really as culturally conformist and conservative as a tall latte from Starbucks.

Any historian worth his salt can see that this "mere Christianity" agenda has a well-established pedigree in Christendom. At the time of the Reformation, Erasmus, writing against Luther, used a combination of Renaissance skepticism, intellectual elitism, and contemporary Catholic teaching on church authority to argue for a Christianity which was essentially practical in orientation and minimally doctrinal in content.[11] In seventeenth-century England, Richard Baxter adopted a linguistic philosophy suggestively akin to that of his contemporary Thomas Hobbes in order to undercut the traditional metaphysical basis of Christian orthodoxy and offer a minimal account of the doctrines of the faith.[12] In the

---

[10] See Quentin Skinner, "Meaning and Understanding in the History of Ideas," in *Visions of Politics I* (Cambridge: Cambridge University Press, 2002), 57–89.

[11] See Bernhard Lohse, *The Theology of Martin Luther* (Edinburgh: T and T Clark, 1999), 162.

[12] See the analysis of the linguistic logic underlying Baxter's ecumenical theology and its impact upon the nature and scope of theological formulation in Carl R. Trueman, "Richard Baxter on

early nineteenth century, Friedrich Schleiermacher responded to Kant's critical philosophy by fusing pietism, Romanticism, and a post-Kantian anti-metaphysical bent to reconstruct Christian doctrines as statements about religious psychology, not transcendent theological truths. And evangelicalism, from its roots in revivalism and pietism, through its development in the pragmatic, anti-speculative culture of America, to its current existence as a more-or-less amorphous, transdenominational coalition, has historically embodied in its very essence an antipathy to precise and comprehensive doctrinal statements.[13] To make the point of immediate relevance in a Westminster context, it was this kind of evangelical position, and not really true liberalism in the technical sense, against which Machen was fighting at Princeton prior to 1929. Therefore, it would seem at least arguable from the perspective of history that the evangelical appropriation of certain aspects of postmodernism is not really a radical break with the past. It might simply be a co-opting of the latest cultural idiom to give trendy and plausible expression to a well-established and traditional ideal of "mere Christianity."[14]

Let me interject a clarification at this point lest I be misinterpreted as saying that mere Christianity is something wrong in itself, a matter to be despised. That is emphatically not what I am saying at all. Salvation does not depend upon the individual's possession of an elaborate doctrinal system or a profound grasp of intricate and complex theology. Yet this is not my point. What I am claiming is that *mere Christianity*, a Christianity which lacks this doctrinal elaboration, is an insufficient basis either for building a church or for guaranteeing the long-term stability of the tradition of the

---

Christian Unity: A Chapter in the Enlightening of English Reformed Orthodoxy" in *Westminster Theological Journal* 61 (1999), 53–71.

[13] The obvious example of this is the reception within evangelical ranks of C. S. Lewis, the impact of whose book, *Mere Christianity*, within American evangelical circles has been immense.

[14] See D. G. Hart, *Defending the Faith: J Gresham Machen and the Crisis of Conservative Protestantism in Modern America* (Grand Rapids: Baker, 1995).

church, i.e. the transmission from generation to generation and from place to place of the faith once for all delivered to the saints. What is disturbing is that the advocates of postmodern mere Christianity are not debating how much one must believe to be saved; they are actually proposing a manifesto for the life of the church as a whole, a somewhat more comprehensive and ambitious project. It is the validity of this that I question.

To return to my main point: eclectic, simplistic, and popularized appropriation of Wittgensteinian linguistics and uncritical engagement with pop culture finds fertile soil in a movement committed not so much to the real implications of Wittgenstein's philosophy of language as to the defusing of the problems faced by a transdenominational movement seeking a place at that oft-mentioned but somewhat nebulous "table." Evangelicalism is, after all, based not upon comprehensive dogmatic formulation but upon a loose collection of elective affinities, only some of which are doctrinal.[15] I would argue, therefore, that seen in this light, the long-term contribution of postmodernism to evangelicalism will ultimately be seen to be more of form than of substance; ho-hum, the singer changes yet again, but, in the words of Led Zeppelin, the song remains the same. This is surely why evangelical expressions of postmodernism are often so tame and uncritical compared to their counterparts in the secular academy, and why they are rarely taken seriously by those outside of the evangelical subculture. In my admittedly limited experience it does not really seem to be the case that postmodern evangelicals want to engage with the truly radical philosophical implications

---

[15] The problems faced with conversions to Roman Catholicism by Wheaton College by its faculty and by the Evangelical Theological Society by its office bearers highlights the problem faced by institutions and organizations with minimal, albeit evangelical, doctrinal bases. In the cases of Joshua Hochschild at Wheaton, and Francis Beckwith in the ETS, both men made good claims to be able to sign the relevant doctrinal bases while yet being good Catholics. In my opinion, their positions were certainly arguable by the letter of the law, even if at odds with its spirit.

of the various postmodern philosophies; it is rather that evangelicals are drawn to the idiom of postmodernism because it facilitates a hip, trendy, and culturally plausible in-house defense of the classic, established evangelical notion of a mere Christianity.[16]

Further, evangelical postmodernism often fails to subject postmodernism itself to any radical critique. Instead, it seems to assume its basic validity as a given and therefore, by implication, as ideologically neutral. Postmodernism's allegedly overwhelming cultural dominance does not, of course, in any way prove its validity; yet one must search hard for any serious post-conservative evangelical discussion of the possibility, articulated so well by Jameson, Anderson, and Eagleton among others, that postmodernism might itself be a highly ideological modernism extended to its absolute limits. The reason for this critical lacuna? To quote Bob Dylan again, you never ask questions with God on your side; and to the extent that postmodernism is the all-embracing, omnipresent, godlike cultural system which imperiously castrates and internalizes all opposition, and to the extent that mere Christianity is the evangelicals' God-given ideal, there is no need to ask the really critical questions.[17] Postmodern

---

[16] For example, I have never come across a self-proclaimed postmodern Christian who regards the biblical prohibition on child sacrifice as being purely contingent and contextual; yet in the university setting where I initially worked as an academic I had numerous friends who regarded child sacrifice as definitely not something one would want to do in the Senior Common Room of a British university but who also regarded any attempt to make that a universal moral imperative, binding on all contemporary societies, as an act of Western imperial hubris. I address some of these issues in my response to Franke's "Reforming Theology" (see note 9 above); I leave it to the reader to decide if his attempt to answer the challenge is a cogent one: see Carl R. Trueman, "It Ain't Necessarily So," *Westminster Theological Journal* 65 (2003), 311–25; John R. Franke "Postmodern and Reformed? A Response to Professors Trueman and Gaffin," *Westminster Theological Journal* 65 (2003), 331–43.

[17] Examples of this abound. Take, for example, the use which the late Stanley Grenz makes of *Star Trek* for understanding. Grenz, who is rare among writers on postmodernism in being able to make the subject accessible and entertaining, certainly makes numerous helpful

evangelicalism, like much of postmodernism, presents itself to the world with all the smug self-importance of a radical revolution. Yet this is an illusion, because the end result at which it aims is as old as the hills, as exclusively doctrinaire as it can be, and as traditional and conservative as it comes: an old-hat, mere Christianity, articulated in a contemporary cultural idiom which actually renders it utterly powerless to challenge the dominant culture and yet impervious to criticism.[18]

THE PROBLEM OF REFORMED ORTHODOXY

This brings me to the issue of Reformed Orthodoxy.[19] The postmodern evangelical literature has little time for Reformed Orthodoxy, typically characterizing it as an example of how

---

observations on how one can track wider cultural changes in society by looking at how humans are portrayed vis-à-vis aliens in the various incarnations of the Star Trek franchise, from the 1960s to the 1990s. Yet he never asks the really interesting questions such as "Who is paying for this?" "Why do they project these images the way they do?" "Why is *Star Trek* on this channel at this particular time of day?" In other words, for all of the criticism of modernism as aspiring to presenting reality as it really is, there is a sense in which Grenz himself operates with the assumption that what is portrayed on *Star Trek* is, in a deep and real sense, a mirror of reality. See Stanley J. Grenz, *A Primer on Postmodernism*, 1–10. The same critical thinking might be applied to *The Simpsons*. Rather than simply worrying about the fact that Ned Flanders is such a pious goof and thus about how the church needs to shed this public image (a most laudable intention with which I have no quarrel!), Christians should first ask if the reason why Christians are portrayed in this way has more to do with the agenda of the scriptwriter or the network than the reality of Christianity in America. It is surely worth a moment's pause to wonder why Fox, the most politically conservative of all stations, chooses to give *The Simpsons* a nightly slot just after dinner time.

[18] The politically disempowering impact of postmodernism is clearly identified by Terry Eagleton: see his *Illusions of Postmodernism* and *After Theory*; by analogy, the same disempowerment applies to theology and to the gospel.

[19] I define Reformed Orthodoxy as that theological movement which arose after the Reformation (ca. 1560 onwards) and sought to

Enlightenment rationalism infected and perverted Christian theology.[20] Yet I would suggest that the real problem which postmodern evangelicalism has with Reformed Orthodoxy is not so much that it is a form of rationalism. That claim can be, and has been, easily debunked time and time again.[21] The claim's persistence as received truth therefore indicates that something else, other than the actual evidence, is keeping it alive. Let me therefore indulge in a moment of speculation: the problem, I suspect, is rather that Reformed Orthodoxy is, well, *orthodox*, that it offers a fairly detailed and extensive account of the Christian faith which stands in clear opposition

---

consolidate the inisights of the earlier Reformers within the wider culture of the university and the church, evidenced particularly in the development of ecclesiastical confessions and catechisms. In addition, in the increasingly complex cultural, polemical, ecclesiastical, and pedagogical environment, Reformed theology during this time underwent considerable doctrinal elaboration, an elaboration which should not be interpreted by misusing categories such as *scholastic* and *rationalism* to explain developments. The major study of doctrinal elaboration during this period is that of Richard A. Muller, *Post Reformation Reformed Dogmatics* (hereafter *PRRD*), 4 vols (Grand Rapids: Baker, 2003).

[20] The portrayal of Reformed Orthodoxy in Grenz and Franke, *Beyond Foundationalism*, is most misleading. For example, while the work of Richard A. Muller is cited on the issue of Scripture, the authors demonstrate no actual knowledge of his argument at all in the way they present Reformed Orthodox approaches to Scriptures as leading to a radical methodological antithesis between Scripture and tradition: see 102–04. Beyond this misuse of Muller, the authors ignore all of the massive volume of scholarship on sixteenth-and seventeenth-century exegesis or theological method which has been produced in this field over the last thirty years, and this critical lacuna in their argument feeds directly into their analysis of the subject.

[21] See Muller, PRRD 1; see also Carl R. Trueman and R. Scott Clark (eds), *Protestant Scholasticism: Essays in Reassessment* (Carlisle: Paternoster, 1999); Willem J Van Asselt and Eef Dekker (eds), *Reformation and Scholasticism: An Ecumenical Enterprise* (Grand Rapids: Baker, 2001); Jeffrey Mallinson, *Faith, Reason, and Revelation in Theodore Beza (1519–1605)* (Oxford: Oxford University Press, 2003); Carl R. Trueman, *The Claims of Truth: John Owen's Trinitarian Theology* (Carlisle, Paternoster, 1997); and Sebastian Rehnman, *Divine Discourse: John Owen's Theological Prolegomena* (Grand Rapids: Baker, 2002).

to the traditional mere Christianity which evangelicals have co-opted the idiom of postmodernism to help them express. Therefore, those postmodern evangelicals who criticize orthodox responses to their positions as being too preoccupied with epistemology are, I think, quite correct: the postmodern evangelical project is not primarily an epistemological one; it is rather one of aesthetic preference, bound up with matters of taste; I speculate, but perhaps postmodern evangelicals simply find distasteful extensive and detailed doctrinal statements which aspire to universal validity; and their epistemology is on the whole simply instrumental to validating such a preference. Indeed, it is arguable that taste is the key to truth these days, a fulfillment of what Friedrich Nietzsche (a much-neglected prophet of postmodernism) anticipated in *Also Sprach Zarathustra*: "And do you tell me, friends, that there is no dispute over taste and tasting? But all life is dispute over taste and tasting!"[22]

Given Westminster's commitment to upholding the Westminster Standards, it is inevitable that the church historians on faculty must justify their existence by fulfilling their role in this larger institutional task. On one level we can

---

[22] "Of the Sublime Men", *Thus Spoke Zarathustra*, trans. R. J. Hollingdale (London: Penguin, 1969), 140. Despite the emphasis in the literature on postmodernism representing a *linguistic* turn, it is also arguable that it represents just as much an *aesthetic* turn, whereby matters of taste become determinative of that which is deemed to be true and good. For example, much of recent antitheism argumentation, such as that of Richard Dawkins or Christopher Hitchens, has emphasized the *distasteful* results of religious commitment in attempting to refute theism as a viable option. On postmodernism as an aesthetic movement, see Terry Eagleton, *The Ideology of the Aesthetic* (Oxford: Blackwell, 1990); also his application of this approach in *Holy Terror* (Oxford: Oxford University Press, 2005). An interesting example of this kind of approach is provided by John R. Franke in his rejoinder to my response to his "Reforming Theology" article (see notes 9 and 17 above). His response starts with objections to my tone, and thus the rhetorical strategy is from the start an aesthetic one which helps to obscure the more substantive issues raised in the initial exchange. In other words, the rejoinder is itself a good example of postmodern idiom: see his "Postmodern and Reformed?"

do this by doing what I have tried to sketch out in the first section of this lecture: by placing the latest cultural trends in the context of history and thus exposing as premature and uncritical all the hype and the hoo-hah that so often surrounds such. A world, and a church, which is hooked on novelty like some cultural equivalent of crack cocaine needs the cold, cynical eye of the historian to stand as a prophetic witness against it. And make no mistake, when it comes to my approach to trendy evangelical claims to epoch-making insights, beneath the cold, cynical exterior of this particular historian beats a heart of stone.

The other level at which we must fulfill our task as Westminster historians is by exposing the incorrect historiography on the basis of which the postmodern evangelical pundits so often dismiss Reformed Orthodoxy as a necessary prelude to asserting their own theological claims. It is to this that we now turn our attention.

The typical picture of Reformed Orthodoxy offered by the popular postmodern evangelical market is that which we find, for example, in a recent volume which offers an analysis of the tradition based upon a very selective examination of the writings of Charles Hodge. The picture that emerges from this slender reading of Hodge is first read back into Turretin and then extrapolated as if normative for the whole of the confessional Reformed tradition. At the same time, an understanding of scholasticism as an essentially rationalist and deductive method is thrown into the mix. Thus a particular picture of Reformed Orthodoxy is transmitted to the pulpits and the bookshops which inform the literate wing of evangelicalism, a picture which is as depressing and pejorative as it is historically inaccurate.[23]

---

[23] The portrayal, and use, of Charles Hodge in Grenz and Franke, *Beyond Foundationalism*, is inaccurate and misleading. For example, the authors state that he basically follows the scholastic paradigm (14). The problem here is that scholastic paradigm, even within Reformed Orthodoxy, could be used to express a significant variation of theological opinions and detailed content; it is a category mistake to confuse scholasticism with content. Further, by eliding the difference between

First, the authors of such works have failed to engage either with the range and complexity of the seventeenth-century sources of Reformed Orthodoxy, or with the problem of historical development, or with the relevant secondary scholarship in the field. Had they done so, they would have realized that, for example, their definition of scholasticism as essentially rationalist is historically untenable. Albert the Great, Thomas Aquinas, John Duns Scotus, William of Occam, Jacob Arminius, Francisco Suarez, John Owen, Johannes Cocceius, Thomas Barlow, Francis Turretin: all were scholastics, yet represent a diverse and, in some cases, mutually exclusive range of epistemologies, philosophies, and theologies. Scholastic method does not demand a particular doctrinal or philosophical position; it is simply a basic way

---

Hodge and the variegated Reformed tradition, it also sets the tone for using Hodge throughout the work as the touchstone of what Reformed Orthodoxy says, thus obviating the need to deal with the variations within that tradition on key doctrinal and hermeneutical issues. More importantly, given the constructive project Grenz and Franke are proposing, this move effectively cuts off the seventeenth century as a possible resource for contemporary theological reflection. None of the major historical work of, say Richard Muller on scholastic method and Reformed Orthodoxy, nor any of the constructive philosophical work of scholars such as Antonie Vos and Paul Helm, both of whom appropriate seventeenth-century Reformed theology for contemporary philosophical and theological projects, is cited, utilized, or even critiqued. Indeed, it is also surprising to see that Grenz and Franke still seems to hold to the long-discredited central dogma theory of divine sovereignty as the structural center of Reformed Orthodoxy: see *Beyond Foundationalism*, 263–64 (where the authors seem unaware that Hodge is actually quoting the Westminster Shorter Catechism on the decrees, a document which clearly gives neither the structural nor the dogmatic significance to the decrees which the authors impute to Hodge). On the fatal flaws in the central dogma theory of Basil Hall, Ernst Bizer, et al, see the following examples of the growing body of literature on this topic: Karl Barth, *Church Dogmatics* 2.2, edited by G W Bromiley and T. F. Torrance (Edinburgh: T and T Clark, 1957), 77–78 (where Barth seems to think that the Reformed Orthodox in practice paid too little attention to predestination, not too much!); also Richard A. Muller, *Christ and the Decree: Christology and Predestination in Reformed Theology from Calvin to Perkins* (Grand Rapids: Baker, 1986).

of arranging, investigating, and describing objects of study, which was developed in the schools (hence it is *scholastic*), and which demands no single philosophical or theological conviction.[24]

Further, the highly contentious assumption that the nineteenth-century Charles Hodge is typical of the Reformed tradition should set the alarm bells ringing. To take those areas in which Hodge is most often used in such literature as being representative of the tradition as a whole, those of epistemology and revelation, it is arguable that these are the very issues where he deviates most significantly from the seventeenth-century confessional tradition. Most telling in this regard is Hodge's failure to pick up on and develop the distinction between archetypal theology (generally, God's infinite knowledge of himself) and ectypal theology (that knowledge of God which is revealed in finite forms to finite creatures), a point on which I myself erred in a discussion of Hodge some years ago.[25] This distinction was formally developed by Francis Junius in the late sixteenth century but it has roots in the voluntarism of late medieval Scotist understandings of God and of how language refers to God.[26]

---

[24] On the definition of scholasticism, see James A. Weisheipl. "Scholastic Method" in *New Catholic Encyclopedia* 12, 1145–46; Richard A. Muller, "The Problem of Protestant Scholasticism" in Van Asselt and Dekker, *Reformation and Scholasticism*, 45–64; Carl R. Trueman and R. Scott Clark, "Introduction" in *Protestant Scholasticism*, xi-xix; also Willem J. Van Asselt and Eef Dekker, "Introduction" in *Reformation and Scholasticism*, 11–43.

[25] See my review of Alister E. McGrath, *A Passion for Truth: The Intellectual Coherence of Evangelicalism* (Downers Grove: InterVarsity Press, 1996) in *Westminster Theological Journal* 59 (1997), 135-38. I still think it is arguable that the content of the distinction is present in Hodge, but the terminology is absent, and any critical impact it has upon his theology is somewhat muted.

[26] Francis Junius, "Tractatus de Vera Theologia," in *D Francisci Junii Opuscula Theologica Selecta*, ed. A. Kuyper (Amsterdam: Brockhaus, 1882), 37–101. The major difference between the Scotist use of this type of distinction and that of the Reformed is that, for Scotists, the epistemological problem is primarily an ontological one which points to the problem of a finite being's knowledge of an infinite being; for

In Reformed theology, the distinction functions in such a way as to delimit human knowledge of God and to underline the fact that theology is utterly dependent upon God's act of condescending to reveal himself. This ensures that theological statements are only apprehensive, not comprehensive, of the truth as it is in God. Language can thus be referential, but there is no simple one-to-one correspondence between human words and divine realities as they exist in God himself. The presence and function of this distinction in, say, the *Leiden Synopsis*, or Francis Turretin, or, later, in Herman Bavinck, denotes a theological sensitivity to the innate weakness of human language when talking of God; and it roots such God-talk not in any true rationalism but in the free, condescending, revelatory acts of God himself. Such language is still referential; and truth still has a nonnegotiable objectivity; but it is not rationalism in any recognizable Enlightenment sense. [27]

Furthermore, the archetype/ectype distinction in fact precludes any possibility of natural theology in the Enlightenment sense. There can be no autonomous knowledge of God built independent of God's continuing, active, sovereign condescension. Thus, the virtual absence of this conceptual distinction in Hodge marks his deviation from the dominant tradition and effectively disqualifies him from being used as

---

the Reformed, the noetic impact of sin is also a fundamental part of the problem.

[27] *Synopsis purioris theologiae*, I.3–4; Francis Turretin, *Institutio* 3.2.6; Herman Bavinck, *Reformed Dogmatics: Prolegomena*, ed. John Bolt (Grand Rapids: Baker), 212 for discussion in the secondary literature, see Muller, *PRRD* 1, 225–38; Willem J. Van Asselt, "The Fundamental Meaning of Theology: Archetypal and Ectypal Theology in Seventeenth-Century Thought" in *Westminster Theological Journal* 64 (2002), 319–35. That Grenz and Franke, *Beyond Foundationalism*, do not address this basic distinction in their critique of Reformed Orthodox views of God renders their analysis inadequate. One cannot dismiss Reformed Orthodoxy on the basis of Charles Hodge: what about the basic work of Amandus Polanus von Polansdorf on prolegomena? Or the summaries of Reformed epistemology found in works such as the *Synopsis purioris theologiae*? To ignore works such as these is fatal to any analysis of the epistemology of Reformed Orthodoxy.

typical on this point. One might also add that the distinction's all-pervading presence in the Reformed Orthodoxy of the seventeenth century makes the latter somewhat less vulnerable to the later Kantian epistemological critique than might otherwise have been the case. Indeed, it is an established historical fact that it was precisely the Arminian rejection of this distinction which left the theology of the Remonstrants peculiarly vulnerable to incursions of rationalism in the later seventeenth and then the eighteenth centuries.[28] To decry Reformed Orthodoxy as a whole as rationalistic and a precursor of the Enlightenment is thus historically indefensible. History shows that it was the Arminians and figures such as John Locke, advocates of an embryonic form of mere Christianity, who ultimately had difficulty in maintaining any semblance of historic orthodoxy.[29]

This is not the only area where Reformed Orthodoxy is habitually misrepresented as a prelude to being rejected. Another frequent allegation is that Reformed Orthodoxy is overly concerned with pedantic doctrinal precision and little else. This may indeed be so in certain individual cases; but, to borrow a thought from the National Rifle Association, doctrines don't kill people; people kill people. Yes, there has been much unpleasantness in the history of Reformed theology, but that is the product of the unpleasantness of theologians rather than any overly dogmatic essence of Reformed Orthodoxy. Indeed, careful historical work can be of benefit here. Indeed, when one looks at those confessions which constitute the ecclesiastical expressions of Reformed Orthodoxy, it is quite amazing at how economical they are, defining very clearly indeed those issues upon which they pronounce, but leaving much scope

---

[28] Van Asselt, "The Fundamental Meaning of Theology," 335.

[29] Indeed, we can see the inroads of rationalism into Reformed Orthodoxy precisely in the work of a man like Richard Baxter whose agenda was the simplification of Orthodoxy: see Trueman, "Richard Baxter on Christian Unity"; idem, "A Small Step Towards Rationalism: The Impact of the Metaphysics of Tommaso Campanella on the Theology of Richard Baxter," in Trueman and Clark (eds), *Protestant Scholasticism*, 147–64.

for legitimate disagreement in areas where they decline to speak. In comparison either to the Canons of Trent or to the Lutheran Book of Concord, Reformed confessions are, on the whole, concise and sparing in their statements.[30] This pattern is repeated in seventeenth-century discussion of fundamental articles (those minimal things which one must believe to be a credible Christian). Again, the Reformed Orthodox lists of such articles are remarkably short. Thus, to reduce the tradition to dry, pedantic, overly elaborate orthodoxy is again historically incorrect.[31]

While on the subject of Reformed Orthodoxy's alleged doctrinalism, it is also worth noting that the sixteenth-and seventeenth-century Reformed were deeply rooted in the ongoing Western theological tradition. There is indeed an irony in the postmodern evangelical accusation that Reformed Orthodoxy involves an arrogant isolation from the wider theological impulses of both West and East. Given that post-conservativism itself frequently seems to articulate views of language, of knowledge, and indeed of God, of Christ, and of divine revelation, which are without orthodox precedent within the bounds of historic Christianity since patristic times,

---

[30] As a source for Reformed confessions, the best collection available is that in E. F. K. Müller, *Die Bekenntnisschriften der reformierten Kirche* (Leipzig: Deichert, 1903), a far more comprehensive collection than that available in Philip Schaff, *The Creeds of Christendom*, 3 vols (Grand Rapids: Baker, 1983). Reading through Müller is an excellent way of seeing the theological unity in cultural and ecclesiastical diversity of the Reformed faith in the sixteenth and seventeenth centuries.

[31] The Reformed Orthodox wrestled long and hard with exactly which items of the Christian creed were necessary to be believed for credible Christian profession and which found expression in the various lists of *fundamental articles* which exist. While there was no confessional consensus on exactly which articles, and how many, should be included, a representative list can be found in Francis Turretin, *Institutes* 1.14.24. On the whole issue of fundamental articles, see Muller, *PRRD* 1, 406–30; Martin I. Klauber, *Between Reformed Scholasticism and Pan-Protestantism: Jean-Alphonse Turretin (1671–1737) and Enlightened Orthodoxy at the Academy of Geneva* (Selinsgrove: Susquehanna University Press, 1994), 165–87.

such criticism begs obvious questions about who exactly it is who is indulging in hubris with regard to the wider Christian tradition.[32]

Nevertheless, to address the matter positively, when one analyzes, say, the work of a figure such as John Owen or George Gillespie or William Perkins or Amandus Polanus von Polansdorf or Gisbertus Voetius or Francis Turretin, one finds in every single case a vast range of historic theological sources being used. The pages of their theologies overflow with citations of rabbis, of patristic authors West and East, of medieval scholastics, from Anselm to Occam, and of contemporary theologians and thinkers, Protestant and Catholic; and their library catalogues confirm the voracious catholicity of their reading habits.[33] Indeed, I have myself

---

[32] See, for example, John R. Franke, *The Character of Theology: A Postconservative Evangelical Approach* (Grand Rapids: Baker, 2005). I am intrigued by the philosophy of language articulated by John R. Franke, which seems to me by and large a popularization of the later Wittgenstein and yet to lack clarity as to whether or not the world is a linguistic construct: this seems to be the thrust of his argument on pp. 23–26, yet the following statement offers qualifications the precise import of which is both crucial and left unclarified by the writer: "[T]he world we experience is mediated in and through our use of language, meaning that *to some extent* the limits of our language constitute the limits of our understanding of the world. Further, since language is a socially construed product of human construction forged in the context of ongoing interactions, conversations, and engagements, words and linguistic conventions do not have timeless and fixed meanings that are independent from their particular usages in human communities and traditions. *In this sense,* language does not represent reality as much as it constitutes reality" (26, emphasis mine). To what extent do the limits of our language constitute the limits of our understanding of the world? What exactly does it mean to say language does not represent reality as much as constitute it? These are questions which Franke does not appear to answer, leaving this reader with the suspicion that he wants to have his cake and eat it too when it comes to language and truth claims.

[33] See Richard A. Muller, "*Ad fontes argumentorum*: The Sources of Reformed Theology in the Seventeenth Century," in idem, *After Calvin: Studies in the Development of a Theological Tradition* (New York:

argued that John Owen's theology needs to be understood as, on one level, a Protestant modification of an essentially Augustinian-Thomistic theology; and the work of Antonie Vos at Utrecht has pointed to the significant dependence of Reformed theology on the metaphysics of Duns Scotus, particularly on discussions of necessity and contingency.[34] Theological sources do not come more catholic, in every sense of the word, than those used by the Reformed. In addition, the classic creedal categories of Trinitarianism and Christology are central to the Reformed Orthodox project, giving a catholic foundation to all Reformed reflection upon God and salvation.[35]

It is true, of course, that Reformed Orthodoxy does break with the established tradition in key areas. For example, the Reformed uniformly reject the medieval notion that Jesus

---

Oxford University Press) 47–62; also Carl R. Trueman, *John Owen: Reformed Catholic, Renaissance Man* (Aldershot: Ashgate, 2007), 5–33. In addition to the various library catalogues for seventeenth-century divines which are extant (e.g. those of Arminius, Baxter, Owen), there is a fascinating work by John Owen's Oxford tutor, Thomas Barlow, which is a recommended basic reading list for theological students at Oxford (presupposing, of course, a BA degree as a prerequisite). Barlow was a vigorously Reformed Orthodox theologian, bishop, and philosopher, and the catholicity of his reading list (together with a marked emphasis upon biblical textual and exegetical works) is most instructive for understanding Reformed Orthodoxy as it really existed: see his *Autoschediasmata de Studio Theologiae; or, Directions for the Choice of Books in the Study of Divinity* (Oxford, 1699).

[34] See Carl R. Trueman, "John Owen's *Dissertation on Divine Justice*: An Exercise in Christocentric Scholasticism," *Calvin Theological Journal* 33 (1998), 87–103; idem, *John Owen*, 58; Rehnman, *Divine Discourse*, 62–64, 181; Antonie Vos, "De kern van de klassieke gereformeerde Theologie," *Kerk en Theologie* 47 (1996), 106–25; idem, "Reformation and Scholasticism" in Van Assselt and Dekker (eds) *Reformation and Scholasticism*, 99–119; also Andreas Beck, "Gisbertus Voetius (1589–1676): Basic Features of His Doctrine of God," *ibid.* 25–26.

[35] See Muller, *Christ and the Decree*; also Trueman, *The Claims of Truth*. My central thesis in this book is that Owen's theology represents a self-conscious attempt to integrate classic, creedal catholic Trinitarianism with anti-Pelagian notions of grace in the context of Reformed Protestantism's modifications of Western Christology.

Christ is mediator only according to his human nature; instead, they insist on mediation according to both natures; and this change is introduced in order to underscore that mediation is the act of a person, not of an impersonal nature. In other words, the more speculative and metaphysical thrust of certain aspects of patristic and medieval theology is tempered by the Reformed emphasis upon the importance of the historical person of the mediator, and the need to do justice to biblical history.[36] Yet even such breaks with tradition arise out of a serious attempt to connect the new insights of the Reformation with longstanding traditions of theological and conceptual discussion. The greatness of seventeenth-century Reformed Orthodoxy, and of the Westminster Seminary tradition which stands in its line, is that it is possible to have one's cake and eat it: all the greatest theology of the church can be co-opted in the process of theological formulation. And it is the role of Westminster's church historians to demonstrate how this catholicity worked itself out in history, and that not in some amorphous relativism or in a mere Christianity but in clear, thorough, and principled confessional formulation and subsequent ecclesiastical life.

Another area where careful historical work can undo much of the misrepresentation of the popular notion of a vast cultural gulf between today and the world of the past is in the whole area of context and contextualization. Now, it is certainly true that we today have a better conceptual vocabulary for reflecting self-consciously upon issues of context; but it is important to note that both the Reformers and their successors were acutely aware of many contextual issues. At a simple level, the theologically driven desire to produce Bible translations and vernacular liturgies bears

---

[36] See the discussions of the Reformed break with medieval Christological paradigms in its insistence on the mediation of Christ according to both natures in Muller, *Christ and the Decree*, 29–33, 142–49; and Trueman, *John Owen*, 80–81. The Reformed Orthodox were quite capable of breaking with tradition when exegesis demanded it; and the result was a theology considerably less speculative than its medieval antecedents.

witness to this; further, sensitivity to context is evidenced by the variation among the Reformers on matters like worship practices, church-state relations, pastoral counseling, and discipline. For example, the existence of Stranger Churches of European exiles in London during the reign of Edward VI indicates a clear awareness of ethnic differences and a repudiation of the "one size fits all" monolithic mentality so often laid at the door of the Reformed Orthodox.[37] And in an era where almost continual political upheaval made exile and geographical displacement into fairly typical experiences for many Protestants, issues related to these points were never far from the surface. Indeed, Calvin spent almost his entire theological career as an exile, and did more than his fair share of theologizing against the background of ethnic tensions between old Genevan families and French immigrants.[38]

In addition to this, one might also add that Reformed Orthodoxy emerged from and was articulated in a variety of European cultures and contexts which were arguably more diverse in terms of political, social, and economic culture and organization than that of the rather uniform McDonald/MTV/Disney-saturated modern West.[39] Even the attempts by Marxist historians such as Christopher Hill to argue that Puritanism appealed to particular class interests now lie in ruins. Careful work over recent decades has demonstrated that religious conviction in the sixteenth and seventeenth centuries cut right across the various categories, ethnic, class,

---

[37] See, for example, Andrew Pettegree, *Foreign Protestant Communities in Sixteenth-Century London* (Oxford: Clarendon Press, 1986).

[38] As yet there is no major study of Calvin and his theology in terms of his context and identity as an exile. Nevertheless, the excellent work of William G. Naphy on the impact of immigration patterns and ethnic tensions on the Genevan Reformation is highly suggestive of work which could be done in this area: see his *Calvin and the Consolidation of the Genevan Reformation* (Manchester: Manchester University Press, 1994); on the Geneva Academy as a European center of learning see Karin Maag, *Seminary or University? the Genevan Academy and Reformed Higher Education* (Aldershot: Scolar Press, 1995).

[39] See, for example, the essays in Karin Maag (ed.), *The Reformation in Eastern and Central Europe* (Aldershot: Scolar Press, 1997).

gender, etc, which later critical theory might anachronistically wish to impose.[40] Again, Westminster church history can make a signal contribution at this point both by emphasizing that problems of context are as old as the Reformed faith itself, and by pointing to the ways in which the Reformed have addressed this issue in the past.[41]

Yet for all of this massive cultural, linguistic, political, social, geographical, and economic diversity in the sixteenth and seventeenth centuries, careful examination of the primary

---

[40] Christopher Hill's writings in this area are extensive, but perhaps the best expression of his Marxist analysis of the English Civil War is his *The World Turned Upside Down* (New York: Viking Press, 1972). His approach has been subject to widespread critique in recent years, where other issues (e.g. religion; Anglo-Scottish politics) have come to take center stage in the analysis: see Conrad Russell, *The Causes of the English Civil War* (Oxford: Clarendon Press, 1990); John Adamson, *The Noble Revolt: The Overthrow of Charles I* (London: Weidenfeld and Nicolson, 2007). Even a history which focuses on "the people" demonstrates that Hill's class-based categories of analysis of seventeenth-century society and religion are too simplistic and fail to do justice to the diversity then in existence: see Diane Purkiss, *The English Civil War: Papists, Gentlewomen, Soldiers, and Witchfinders in the Birth of Modern Britain* (New York: Basic Books, 2006).

[41] Some may object that, in fact, the patterns of immigration, etc which the West has experienced over the last century or so do radicalize the diversity of society in an unprecedented way. For example, many of us now have Jewish, Moslem, and Hindu neighbors, etc in a way that would have been impossible in the sixteenth century. This is certainly true but I would offer two thoughts by way of laying the foundation for response. First, these differences must be set against the background of a vast amount of common popular culture "glue" which often creates a deeper unity than these other phenomena might suggest (e.g. sports teams, TV programs, commercial chains, designer labels, etc); and also that the situation on the ground in the sixteenth and seventeenth centuries was more diverse than can be ascertained through a study of elite cultural patterns, artifacts, and practices. Take for example, the work of Margo Todd whose study of kirk session records in the early modern period reveals a much more complicated world at grass roots level in the church in the sixteenth and seventeenth centuries than an exclusive focus on published literary texts would suggest: see *The Culture of Protestantism in Early Modern Scotland* (New Haven: Yale University Press, 2002).

texts of Reformed Orthodoxy, whether Scottish or Hungarian, whether by an aristocratic Episcopalian, such as Daniel Featley, or a down-at-heel tinker, such as John Bunyan, reveals through the diversity a remarkably coherent and unified voice. The basics of the gospel and the Reformed faith were actually understood in astoundingly consistent ways across national, linguistic, cultural, and economic boundaries. Further, it is clear that this was not simply a coincidental unity, but arose from the positive, self-conscious conviction of its various advocates that they did indeed speak with a substantially unified voice. Again, historians are well-placed to explain how this was possible.

Any historically attuned study of Reformed Orthodoxy will see that the seventeenth-century theologians of, say, the Westminster Assembly clearly understood humanity, made in the image of God, as a universal. Human beings were not simply cultural constructs, despite all of the diversity that existed between people of different cultures. It was this belief in human nature that then allowed the Reformed to set context, as it were, in context. While the French spoke French and lived under an increasingly absolutist Catholic monarchy, and the English spoke English and established a Puritan commonwealth, and the Dutch spoke Dutch and organized society itself along ecclesiastical-confessional lines, the shared human nature of each of these national groups provided an ultimately unified horizon. This meant that communication was possible between such disparate groups, and that theological content, while only ever occurring in specific space-time contexts, was never reducible to, or bounded by, such contexts. Culture was an artifact of human beings made in the image of God. Human nature thus logically preceded culture and provided the ultimate created context for all other contexts.

The other universal pole was the ectypal, revealed theology of which we have already spoken: God's revelation was just that—a revelation of God, not an expression of the psychological self-consciousness of the religious individual or community. Taken together, the human knower and the divine known provided a fusion of shared, universal horizons which had logical and methodological priority over all other particular contexts. The hyper-Kantian move of dissolving everything, even the human self, into language was—and, one might add, is—anathema to Reformed Orthodox theology. This is why claims that the opening lines of Calvin's *Institutes* offer a principle and a precedent for a postmodern contextual reconstruction of Reformed theology miss the point, both historically and theologically. What Calvin is saying in *Institutes* I.i is that our knowledge of who we are is intimately connected to our knowledge of God and *vice versa*. If he is making a claim about context at all, it is that God, and God's image in us, is the ultimate context for understanding God and humanity and the relationship which exists between them; he is not suggesting that "in the discipline of theology we must take account of the particular social and intellectual settings in which we engage in theological reflection and exploration." Important as these are, it is not what Calvin teaches in *Institutes* I.i. [42]

There is much more that could be said about the misrepresentation of Reformed Orthodoxy in contemporary evangelical presentations: for example, I could address the typical allegation that the Reformed were proof texters who did not understand the nature of exegesis or canonical formation. I have, you will be relieved to know, no time today to deal with this in detail. Suffice it to say that the seventeenth century was the golden age of Protestant linguistics, of biblical commentary, of thoughtful sifting and collating of traditions of exegesis, and of careful attention to the relationship between exegetical work and doctrinal formulation. [43] Again,

---

[42] *Contra* Franke, *The Character of Theology*, 13–14.

[43] On this, see the forthcoming essays on the exegetical methods of the Westminster Divines in Richard A. Muller and Rowland S. Ward, *Scripture and Worship: Biblical Intrepretation and the Directory for Worship* (Phillipsburg: Presbyterian and Reformed, forthcoming). For an example of the integration of dogmatic, traditionary, and exegetical concerns in doctrinal formulation, see my discussion of the covenant of redemption: *John Owen*, 80–87.

underlying all this was a commitment to Scripture as ectypal theology, as the revelation of the one God speaking one message through finite human words. This commitment demanded the development of such linguistic and textual studies, yet it also controlled and regulated those studies in a way that made normative theological formulation possible, indeed imperative for the well-being of the church. Criticism of alleged Reformed Orthodox proof texting by modern authors who themselves engage in almost no biblical exegesis as they offer their alternatives does raise obvious questions again about the difference between what is apparently being said and what is really being done. One might perhaps argue with some justification that the game being played today by post-conservative pundits is not so much that of challenging orthodox exegesis as that of questioning the very notion that it is actually possible to make ecclesiastically normative theological statements on the basis of Scripture. But that is a long story, and one to be saved for another day. Suffice it to say that Westminster church historians are charged with making sure that the historiography behind such arguments is gently but firmly exposed for the illusion that it is.

CONCLUSION

There is a line in one of The Who's greatest songs, "Who are you?" which goes as follows: "I remember throwing punches around and preaching from my chair." I do hope that when I look back on my inaugural day in years to come, my memories will be a little more positive than that. Yet, it is part and parcel of being an academic, particularly at an institution such as Westminster, that one should throw some punches around and use one's chair as a place from which to preach. Indeed, I hope that I have today been quite polemical at points; yet critical thinking and scholarly engagement necessarily require polemic; and such polemic is ultimately a positive, a healthy, and a vital exercise.

Will Westminster church history win a hearing in the wider evangelical culture? Possibly not. After all, the wider evangelical culture has drunk deeply at the anti-historical wells of the contemporary American scene. The task of history itself is thus one which finds little or no natural sympathy in today's world. In addition, the study of Reformed Orthodoxy requires that we do justice to its sophistication, its nuances, its catholicity, its failure to conform to the expected clichés of postmodern consumerism. With the best will in the world, these are not particularly marketable qualities. Thus, I suspect that those who declare confessional Reformed theology to be some species of, say, rationalism, proof textism, and/or ahistorical dogmatism, will continue to shape its popular image. After all, they tell a story which sells books, a nice, simple, straightforward story which confirms the popular belief in the superiority of a pragmatic, anodyne, merely Christian present that needs to forget its past and move on. That this story is told with a necessarily light scholarly apparatus and is demonstrably untrue in its principal historical claims is not a particular problem: it says what people want to hear; it is buoyed along by strong cultural currents; like postmodernism itself, it speciously hides its conservatism under the language of radicalism; and it has the advantage that those books which tell the true story of Reformed Orthodoxy are not themselves easy reading.

Yet the Westminster church history department will never cede cheap ground to the arrivistes of evangelical historiography or to the aesthetics of the contemporary postmodern evangelical world. And, while it may salve the surprisingly sensitive aesthetic consciences of some such to convince themselves that our critiques are simply in bad taste, nothing more than the routine rants of rabid Reformed rottweilers, this is simply not the case. Not at all. I am most happy to acknowledge that the issues which the postmodern evangelicals are addressing and the questions they are asking are very important and need to be addressed with thought and not dismissed out of hand; but these things can only be done in any sound or effective manner on the basis of careful and precise historiography. One cannot critique the inadequacies of the past until one has understood the past; one certainly should not abandon the past on the basis of a caricature; and the kind of historical misrepresentations which undergird certain post-conservative analyses of the tradition stand at odds both with the possibility of such critique and with the claims of the very same people that we need to engage with tradition in order to meet the challenges of the contemporary world. Thus, let me put this as precisely as I can: the vigor of my criticism of such writers is provoked as much by their seriously problematic historiography as by any serious heterodoxy within their theology; indeed, the careful reader will note that I do not offer any criticism of their theology as that is beyond the scope of this lecture.

This message is unlikely to prove popular in some quarters of the evangelical world, but that is of little consequence. Neither I nor my colleagues in the department do what we do in order to be well-liked, popular, or successful; rather, we do what we do because we simply refuse to allow to go unchallenged the received mythology concerning the evils of Reformed Orthodoxy; we do what we do because we love the Reformed faith as much as we dislike shoddy historical writing; we do what we do to make our own small contribution to criticism of the bland aesthetic tastes of modern evangelical theology; and, above all, we do what we do because to remain silent at such a time as this would be to abdicate our moral responsibility to the church. In short, we do it because it is right for us to do so. The light may well be dying, but we will rage, rage against it; and be assured, we will never go gentle into that good night.

UNEASY CONSCIENCES AND CRITICAL MINDS: WHAT THE FOLLOWERS OF CARL HENRY CAN LEARN FROM EDWARD SAID[1]

Carl Trueman

The year 2003 saw the death of two men whose writings have interested me over the years: Edward Said, the great Palestinian literary critic and political activist died of leukaemia in September; and Carl Henry, one of the founding fathers of the new evangelicalism died in December.

To anyone familiar with their work, they seem like strange bedfellows for any one person to link together in this way. Said was a polymathic scholar who also wrote widely on Middle Eastern affairs in a passionate and engaged way; Henry was a high-class journalist who, though undoubtedly very clever and accomplished, really devoted much of his life to a popular explication and application of the Christian faith in the contemporary world. Yet, like other "heroes" of mine, from George Orwell to Alexander Solzhenitsyn, they both represented an ideal: the engaged intellectual; those who saw both the importance of being what one might call informed amateurs in areas which were not within their own

---

[1] I am grateful for comments on this paper by colleagues and friends, especially Bill Edgar, Manny Ortiz, Rob Burns, and Ian Glover.

immediate fields of technical expertise. They responded to the need to speak out uncomfortable truths to those who hold institutional power, whether on the international, national, or local stage. I want to say more about the importance of engaged intellectuals later, but first it is probably wise to introduce Henry in context to those readers unfamiliar with the history and culture of American evangelicalism.

When Carl Henry died on December 7, 2003, aged 90, the world of evangelicalism lost the man who was undoubtedly its elder statesman, one whom Timothy George describes (with forgivable hyperbole) as the man who was central to the very invention of evangelicalism.[2] Certainly, Henry was a remarkable figure, the epitome of the American can-do mentality applied to the areas of evangelical theology and evangelism. Here are just a few of his achievements: he was a member of the founding faculty of Fuller Theological Seminary; the first editor of *Christianity Today*; lecturer at large for World Vision; mentor to Charles Colson; and, through his writings, popularizer and defender of evangelical orthodoxy, particularly on the issue of Scripture through his six volume work, *God, Revelation, and Authority* (1976–83; recently republished by Paternoster). Like John Stott or Martyn Lloyd Jones in the UK, he was one of the men who set some of the basic agenda for evangelical life in the post-war US.

While Henry did work on the international stage, he was, as the short summary above indicates, essentially an American figure. It seems therefore appropriate to spend a few pages of *Themelios* introducing him to our predominantly British (or at least non-American) readership. This will facilitate a better understanding both of the man and his work and of the current state of American evangelicalism. Whether we like it or not, America sets the agenda here as in so many other areas. After all, American evangelical books fill study shelves around the world; and the larger culture of America has marked life in all parts of the globe. Understanding America

---

[2] "Inventing Evangelicalism," *Christianity Today*, March 2004; available at www.christianitytoday.com/ct/2004/003/6.48.html

is therefore important if only because even those who are most vigorously anti-American still define themselves in terms set by the USA.

To assess simultaneously both the contribution of Carl Henry and the culture of American evangelicalism is no easy task, and I will attempt no exhaustive presentation here. Instead, I have decided to take as my guide Henry's little book from 1947, *The Uneasy Conscience of Modern Fundamentalism*. Though less than 100 pages in total, it was the work which brought Henry to national prominence and for which he will, in the long run, probably be best remembered.[3]

To understand the book, it is important to grasp something of the nature of American fundamentalism (basically a synonym for evangelicalism prior to the movement to which Henry belonged) in the 1930s. Essentially, the movement was characterized by a cultural and moral legalism, opposed, for example, to Hollywood, cinema, dancing, consumption of alcohol, and smoking (at least in the northern states whose economy did not depend upon tobacco). There was also an intellectual and theological obscurantism, where learning was regarded with deep suspicion. Both the legalism and the obscurantism were reinforced by a deep-rooted dispensational theology. When one combined these with public relations disasters such as Prohibition and the Scopes Trial, the evangelical world in which Henry cut his teeth in the thirties and forties was marked by its basic irrelevance to American society. It simply had nothing of any interest to say to the modern world.[4]

It was against this background that a group of younger evangelicals, including Carl Henry, along with others such as E. J. Carnell, George Eldon Ladd, and Paul K. Jewett,

---

[3] The work has recently been republished, with a new introduction by the current President of Fuller, Richard Mouw, and the original introduction by Harold Ockenga, by Eerdmans (2003).

[4] Good introductions to this period are George Marsden, *Fundamentalism and American Culture: The Shaping of Twentieth Century Evangelicalism 1870–1925* (Oxford: OUP, 1980); D. G. Hart, *Defending the Faith: J Gresham Machen* (Grand Rapids: Baker, 1995).

decided to launch a revised evangelicalism, indeed, a "new evangelicalism" in post-World War II America. They obtained degrees from mainstream universities; they addressed themselves to the latest developments in theology and biblical studies. They also sought to defend and expound Christian evangelical orthodoxy in a way that avoided the vicious polemical tone of the past.[5]

The agenda for this new movement was nowhere expressed more clearly, nor in briefer compass, than in Henry's book, *Uneasy Conscience*. In eight brief chapters, Henry offered very little in the way of specific suggestions for action and much in the way of general, inspiring rhetoric to goad his fellow evangelicals out of their social, cultural, and political apathy and mobilize them for activism in all these fields. The major problem, as Henry saw it, is a basic indifference to the world around engendered by an indifference to the present, something which is intimately related to the faulty eschatology of dispensationalism. To quote Henry himself, "Whereas once the redemptive gospel was a world-changing message, now it was narrowed to a world-resisting message" (p. 19). What evangelicals needed to grasp was the fact that their message applied to all of life, and was transformative of all areas of human endeavor. They should therefore prepare themselves accordingly. Whether consciously or unconsciously, Henry seemed to know that the development of this program required the development of a distinctive evangelical consciousness, and that required the production of the necessary cultural tools (68–71). Such could only be achieved by the proper education of leaders to manage these tools, and the creation of a popular evangelical front which set aside divisive secondary doctrines in favor of maintaining a unified policy in the face of the common secularizing foe.

In light of this manifesto, we can see Henry's time at Fuller, his work on *Christianity Today*, his involvement with the Evangelical Theological Society, and his various other activities

---

[5] On the atmosphere and agenda of the new evangelicals, see George Marsden, *Reforming Fundamentalism: Fuller Seminary and the New Evangelicalism* (Grand Rapids: Eerdmans, 1987).

on the evangelical stage, as part and parcel of his desire to see evangelicalism making a difference to the world around by engaging thoughtfully and relevantly with the world as it presented itself. On the occasion of his death, therefore, it seems appropriate to ask to what extent the project has proved successful, and whether we can learn from the strengths and weaknesses which it embodied.

Before doing so, however, it is important for me to state clearly my own position relative to the American evangelical scene so as to allow the reader the opportunity to play "spot the prejudice" in my own analysis. I am, according to the US Immigration and Naturalization Service, a "non-resident alien"; in other words, I live in America (and, indeed, I find that, generally speaking, I like living in America) but I do not belong to America; and that is a useful way of understanding my take on American evangelicalism. It is the world I inhabit, but I do not belong there, and thus perhaps have the ability to spot certain things which a native might miss through overfamiliarity. There is also the potential to misunderstand other things for precisely the same reasons. I am also familiar with only a relatively narrow band of American Christian life, that is, the white Reformed, generally suburban/urban professional middle-class branch. Of Mennonite, Arminian, African American, and Latino streams, to name but four, my knowledge is limited and mainly second hand. Yet this places me very close to the kind of evangelicals to whom Henry was making his appeal.

The first comment to make about Henry's book is that it is first and foremost a plea for evangelical engagement with society and culture at all levels. This is not to say that Henry is laying out a detailed plan of what such an engagement should look like. Unlike many of the current generation of American evangelicals, Henry, though clearly something of a Republican himself, stopped well short of identifying a particular brand of politics as being distinctively Christian, preferring instead to argue that Christians should be *involved*, not prescribing exactly what that involvement should look like. The dilemma he faced was this: on the one hand, those Christians who engaged in politics, the arts, etc. were on the whole those of definite liberal or neo-orthodox convictions which gave the whole arena of cultural engagements a somewhat heterodox feel. On the other hand, the fundamentalists, particularly as influenced by the "pull up the drawbridge and wait for the end" mentality of dispensationalism, had tended to regard any engagement with the world as futile. Any attempt to improve the social, political, and cultural spheres was, at best, pointless and naïve, at worst "worldly" and positively sinful. In the late forties, of course, with the Iron Curtain, the Berlin crisis, and the increasing anti-Red hysteria of American politics, this mentality was reinforced by a knee-jerk fear of anything which smacked of socialism.

Over against this, Henry argued that evangelical Christianity had developed a faulty eschatology which projected Christ's kingdom into the future and thus had lost sight of the nature of that kingdom in the present day and age. Eschatology became the reason—or perhaps the pretext—for retreating from fields of necessary Christian endeavor. One can understand the attraction of this. The collapse of orthodoxy in the mainline denominations in the 1920s, coupled with the various social forces unleashed by the economic policies of the 1930s and the trauma of the Second World War and the start of the Cold War, meant that many of the old certainties, whether social, political, or theological, were no longer as impregnable as they had once seemed. Retreat in such circumstances must have seemed most attractive; and baptizing that retreat with a theological rationale which made it appear biblical must have had tremendous appeal. Like the boy in the schoolyard who has been excluded from the soccer match and who then turns away in tears declaring that he never wanted to play anyway, so fundamentalist Christianity turned from the traditional public sphere and retreated into its own subculture.

Since Henry's day, of course, much has changed, and that in no small measure because of the life and work of Henry himself. Indeed, if we look at just two areas, those of theological and political engagement, we can see the difference that the kind of vision encapsulated in Henry's manifesto and pioneered by him and his colleagues has made to the American evangelical world.

THEOLOGICAL ENGAGEMENT

Henry's own life and work, supremely the six volumes of *God, Revelation and Authority (GRA)*, indicate how seriously he took the need to work out evangelical orthodoxy in a contemporary context. There are times when this gives his work a bizarre and very dated feel—for example, the long interaction in GRA with the "Jesus People" who have proved about as significant for Christianity since the 1960s as Rolf Harris's Stylophone has been for the music of Kraftwerk. Nevertheless, the central point of these volumes is that scriptural authority is significant, that it is not enough to say the Bible is true or authoritative without defining such notions with great care and relating them to other theological points, and that this must be done in a manner which is relevant to the challenges of today, not yesterday. And this point is well-made and well-taken. Indeed, one could argue that it was this issue, the relation between God, revelation, and Scripture, that dominated much of Henry's early and mid-career. This was reflective of a more general concern in the wider theological world from the 1940s through 1960s with the problem of what exactly constituted revelation. Of course, it is always relevant; but it had peculiar relevance at this point in time, and Henry's response indicated his sensitivity to the times.

Nevertheless, while Henry's dream of articulating evangelical theology in a thoughtful, nuanced way is admirable, the practical realities of the vision were flawed. The institutions which spearheaded the new evangelicalism (Fuller Seminary, *Christianity Today*, the Evangelical Theological Society) were all interdenominational in order to produce a kind of popular front evangelicalism, focused on gospel essentials. This was done in order to combat the forces of theological liberalism and, to a much lesser extent, of fundamentalism.[6] Such a

---

[6] It is interesting that Henry's criticisms of fundamentalism in *Uneasy Conscience* are carefully nuanced to ensure that there is no doubt

vision is admirable, arguably representing an attempt to take seriously New Testament teaching on the unity of all believers in Christ. Britain has its parallel institutions: the old London Bible College (now the London School of Theology); UCCF; the Evangelical Alliance; the British Evangelical Council (now Affinity). While the origins and agendas of these British groups differ somewhat from their American counterparts, the vision of a popular evangelical front is much the same. Yet the strength of this model—that of transcending traditional, denominational boundaries—is also its weakness, in that it removes the activity of theology from the immediate church context. This has a twofold effect: first, it can foster a somewhat eclectic approach to theology, with a marginalizing of areas where disagreement exists, regardless of how important they are; and, second, it removes the obvious mechanisms of accountability.

To take the first of these. The sidelining of issues which historically divide evangelicals can be a most positive thing. Should differing views of baptism, say, or eschatology, prevent informal fellowship between believers and churches in different traditions, or hinder joint evangelistic campaigns? Most are inclined to say not, as this might lead to a complete fragmentation of evangelicalism which would inevitably undermine effectiveness. Yet this raises the problem of which issues are central and which are peripheral. Given that many died on both sides of the eucharistic debate at the Reformation, should we see different views of the Lord's Supper as mere superficial differences or as disagreements which must disrupt all fellowship? Perhaps a more pertinent example for modern evangelicalism would be the disagreement between Calvinists and Arminians over the nature of human decision with reference to salvation, or between charismatics and non-charismatics with reference to the continuation or cessation of the spiritual gifts. To what extent are differences significant?

---

in the reader's mind that, while theological liberalism is the enemy, fundamentalism has more the character of a misguided friend. He clearly saw it as having a grasp of the supernatural gospel, albeit in a somewhat truncated form, in a way that liberalism simply did not.

It is tempting to argue that the answer to this question really depends upon the circumstances. Sharing a platform in the interests of a local evangelistic campaign with others with whom one disagrees on these issues would seem, all else being equal, an appropriate, modest, and charitable position to take, one which avoids the nasty excesses of narrow sectarianism. I would wish, at this point, to stress my agreement with such an attitude, allowing as it does for a manifestation of the heart of the gospel and a focusing of minds on that which unites, rather than that which divides. Yet here is the problem: who, in these circumstances, decides where the boundaries are to be drawn at each level of possible co-operation? On what basis do they do so (from, say, a common platform against abortion, where Protestants routinely speak with Roman Catholics, and even, on occasion, atheists and representatives of other religions—again, legitimately in many instances in my opinion—to a joint communion service or agreements regarding mutual eligibility of ministers)? Thus, the broad-based nature of evangelicalism is both its greatest strength and its most unfortunate weakness.

The most graphic example of this problem in action has been the events surrounding the debate over the openness of God which has taken place in the Evangelical Theological Society. Here certain orthodox evangelicals made an attempt to rule that openness teaching was in conflict with the Society's position and that those holding to such should cease to be members. My own very personal take on this issue is twofold: I do not regard open theism as Christian orthodoxy and therefore see it as having no place in a Christian organization. Yet, given the fact that the ETS is not a church and that its doctrinal basis of membership only requires belief in inerrancy and in a basic Trinitarianism, I see no constitutional grounds for the expulsion of individuals who sign this and believe it. The key issues for me theologically (e.g. divine foreknowledge, penal substitution, the nature of grace) are simply not dealt with in the Doctrinal Basis, inferential arguments from inerrancy notwithstanding. Therein lies the problem: transdenominational organizations need to play down differences in order to function; yet in so doing they raise questions about the drawing of boundaries which cannot be easily answered.

This, yet again, brings us to the issue of accountability: who decides what the limits of fellowship are in these transdenominational organizations? Where doctrinal bases exist, who decides where the lines must be drawn or what can and cannot be embraced within them?

To deal with this in any detail would be too complex, but one significant issue which is often missed in discussion and which relates very closely to the way in which evangelicalism connects to American culture, is the need of these groups to raise money. Evangelicalism is costly: from the glossy pages of *Christianity Today*, to the payrolls of the seminaries, to the lecture fees of evangelical superstars, evangelicalism needs money. And in practice this means that its public position is always a negotiation between various theological concerns and the willingness of those with money to underwrite the project. This is where the problems of accountability can become acute. Even the briefest glance at the pages of *CT* reveals how much the organ depends upon advertising for revenue; and this dependence is not theologically neutral.

First, the kinds of ads carried are, by virtue of being in the pages of *CT*, invested with the authority of the magazine, whatever the editor might claim to the contrary. Editors may not personally approve of a particular product (and, one might add in passing that the existence of advertising for theology courses and books does turn theology into a product to be packaged, branded, and sold—itself an interesting phenomenon); but allowing them to be placed in their journal gives them formal approval. I should know, as I edit the journal you are currently reading, which, as you notice, carries almost no advertising as a matter of principle. When adverts for a veritable smorgasbord of seminaries appear in the pages of *CT*, the differences between them are inevitably relativized by virtue of their existence as part of the larger consensus being created by the magazine itself. When advertisements for Christian approaches to financial security appear in the pages of *CT*, placing personal wealth near the top of Christian priorities, then *CT*, and the evangelicalism it claims to represent, surrenders any possibility of compelling prophetic critique of the prosperity gospel within its pages.

Second, companies only place advertisements in organs that sell; so sales become very important; and this means that the editor needs to maintain circulation in order to maintain commercial income. Thus there will be a constant pressure to make sure that the content of the journal appeals to the widest range of readers possible. This almost certainly means a lowering of the intellectual level in order to net as big an audience as possible. Any comparison of the *CT* of Henry's day with that of ours would seem to confirm that the magazine has become glossier, more aesthetic, and less intellectually demanding, as the years have gone by. This is surely not unrelated to the way in which it is financed and marketed. As commercial television is more likely to succeed by producing "reality TV" instead of documentaries on AIDS in sub-Saharan Africa, so *Christianity Today* is more likely to maintain circulation by running interviews with Max Lucado than with some less photogenic character doing something less exciting than writing bestsellers. One might also note that when the organs which help to create and sustain the unity of one's movement are dependent upon the consumerist system of Western society, it becomes very difficult to mount any effective critique of, or resistance to, that system. It becomes internalized, as unquestioned as the laws of gravity.

Third, given the transdenominational disparate nature of the evangelical world noted above, the very function of a media organ such as *Christianity Today* is in large part to manufacture a kind of consensus. It is to create at least the appearance of unity among dramatically different groupings. This places at the heart of the new evangelical project a natural gravitational pull towards lowest common denominator themes. In turn this influences the mindsets of those who read the organ uncritically and with no awareness that the very nature of a commercial media product as such is somewhat less than ideologically neutral. Organs such as *CT* do not simply reflect the evangelical world; they create it. In a certain sense they determine who and what gets covered, and the demands of consensus and commerce mean that certain figures will get better coverage than others.

This is not to say that these problems could be solved by dismantling transdenominational evangelical enterprises *tout court*. I suspect such would be disastrous and would militate against the Bible's teaching on the unity of the body. I would argue that Henry's vision needs to be modified, indeed radicalized, to include careful reflection upon how evangelicalism is to be held accountable to the church. I would also argue that it does not simply need to engage with society but that it also needs to subject the most unspoken orthodoxies of modern Western society to vigorous critique. It is this which the political engagement of the white middle-class American evangelicalism has, on the whole, failed to do in any radical sense.

Political Engagement

If the fundamentalism against which Henry was reacting was politically apathetic, looking for a kingdom which was projected pretty much into the future, much of white American evangelicalism today is tied to right-wing politics of a fairly radical kind. Economically there is little to choose between Republican and Democratic options at the ballot box. One is dealing with debates about the weighting of tax burdens, with the basic free market system being an unquestioned orthodoxy for both parties. There are some key areas of disagreement on foreign policy, but the real division for many Christians is the issue of abortion.[7] Although reports seem to

---

[7] To be fair, the content of *World* magazine, whose readership is overwhelmingly white, would seem to indicate that other issues are starting to come to the fore, especially education (i.e. creationism; home-schooling) and family values (i.e. gay marriage). *World* is without doubt one of the principle means by which an apparent political consensus on a host of other issues (welfare, foreign policy, etc) has been created and sustained as normative orthodoxy among an influential segment of middle-class white conservative evangelicals in the USA.

indicate that substantial minorities in both parties disagree with their official party lines (Republicans are pro-life; Democrats are pro-choice), this does not translate into grass roots nuancing of political allegiances. There is a fierce loyalty to the Republicans being exhibited by most white Christians. Henry himself in *Uneasy Conscience* was careful to avoid the identification of any economic system with Christianity (e.g. 84–85). The current function, however, of abortion as the card which trumps everything has killed meaningful political thinking on other issues in many evangelical circles. Health care, foreign policy, and welfare are simply non-issues when compared to the termination of pregnancies. Eschatology is perhaps less significant, but US policy towards Israel is undoubtedly shaped to some extent by the power of groups which hold to a particular view of the role of the restoration of political Israel at the end of time. This is reinforced at a grass-roots level by the popularity of the end-times novels of Tim LaHaye and Jerry Jenkins, a popularity which is not restricted simply to Christians.

Underlying this is something that is perhaps more insidious. That is the belief among many American evangelicals that America has a special place in God's providential care. This is, of course, the archetypal error which all dominant political and economic powers have made, from Rome (see Augustine's *City of God*) to the British Empire. Yet America is so all-surpassingly powerful on the world stage. The language of manifest destiny is so deeply ingrained in her public discourse, from the mythologies of the Founding Fathers to those of Hollywood. Nationalism, intensified by being connected with the language of divine sanction, is a very real problem. The myth of American superiority in all areas is one which the popular media perpetuate by playing up America's undoubted strengths while ignoring her weaknesses and the contributions of other countries and societies. Even the allegedly liberal minded in Hollywood are deeply involved in this mythologizing of America—witness films such as *The Last Samurai*. And then the cult of strength, beauty, and superiority is long-established. Back in the 1930s George Orwell expressed concern that no ugly or poor people were generally allowed to spoil the aesthetics of American magazines and newspapers. Today the television provides an even more powerful way of reinforcing such national mythology. The myth of American superiority has also produced the perfect antibody for dealing with the microbes of criticism: any criticism can be seen as motivated by envy at American success and is thus actually more evidence of the superiority of the American way.

The American church should be ideally placed to act as the nation's conscience at this time, the role which Henry seemed to wish it to play in his manifesto. Yet too many churches are committed to being part of the myth rather than being the prophetic critics of the same. As if to symbolize this collusion, in many churches the American flag stands next to the pulpit. This is something which, in my experience of travel around the world, is a somewhat unique juxtaposition. It is bizarre given the constitutional commitment to separation of church and state. What is more, the American way is routinely identified with God's will in sermons and on Christian television, sometimes in a rather worryingly direct fashion. Indeed, I have a colleague who prayed for world peace at a recent service and was admonished for praying an "unAmerican" prayer. The fact that there is such a term as "unAmerican" is itself interesting. There is no real equivalent as far as I know in other countries with which I am familiar: what would "unDutch" or "unBritish" mean, I wonder? This is because "American" is not a term which speaks primarily of a geographical location or a birthplace but rather of a set of values. Such values can be defined in various ways; but, however that may be done, "unAmerican" is regarded by all as a pejorative. That it can be used in a church context about a prayer for peace gives one worrying pause for thought. That these values can become implicitly (and often explicitly) nothing less than an eschatology is extremely disturbing.

The identification of America and the American way, with its freedom, democracy, and free market philosophy, as identical with God's way probably owes much, at a sophisticated level, to the influence of the secular political mythologies of neo-

Hegelians such as Fukuyama on certain leading Christian opinion-formers; at a popular level, I suspect the culprit is a basic human pride in anything that allows one to feel superior to others. That certain strands of evangelicalism have bought into this identification of right-wing politics, the American way, and Christianity big time should be a cause for concern. Henry's call was for evangelicalism to take on a *prophetic* role, one of being involved in the political process but in such a manner that the politics of the secular world were not to be identified wholesale with the gospel. It was not to be there simply to baptize the politics of one party rather than another.

The relationship between the church and politics is always going to be complicated. This is not least because political thinking is a culturally specific, occasional activity, where the black and white moral categories of right and wrong do not always, or even often, apply. After all, every Christian who takes the Bible seriously should hate poverty and want the innocent protected from the violent and the oppressive. But is it necessarily sinful to believe that this is best achieved through free markets or through nationalized industries, or through particular configurations of tax burdens and welfare payments? Is one health care system biblical and another unbiblical? Only the crudest of Bible-thumping simpletons can possibly correlate the teaching of the Bible in a direct, no-nonsense way with the party political platforms of the early twenty-first century. British evangelicals need to remember this as they become increasingly active in their political involvement. They also need to be aware of the fact that the claiming of divine sanction for opinions which are, in themselves, morally indifferent or at least debatable, is the oldest trick in the book for foreclosing on intelligent discussion. Even black and white issues are not so black and white when it comes to specific party politics. Yes, God hates the slaughter of infants—but abortion is merely the most obvious way in which this takes place. Poor healthcare, unhygienic living conditions, lack of access to AIDS drugs, famine, sweatshops, unemployment, underemployment, war, environmental damage due to pollution and greed—these all kill infants too.

Reflection on these makes party politics less black and white than many would wish. It is time for Christians to face up to these issues as well.

Looking at the world of 2004, one can therefore say that part of Henry's dream has been fulfilled: a professing Christian is in the White House; and evangelicals are involved in the formation of public policy. Yet the black and white, simplistic politics that have come to dominate large swathes of white evangelicalism in America are scarcely those for which Henry hoped. Modern American evangelicalism has neither critiqued nor transformed the political landscape. Instead it has largely bought into the polarized politics of the two party system and lost its ability to be critical of the American way. It has, if you like, become too worldly. Henry's original vision for politics has only partly been realized; and, lest this seem like more hackneyed America-bashing, let me stress that I say this because I like the country in which I now live and I long to see the church there become as strong spiritually and evangelistically as it is numerically.

This, of course, is the final problem with regarding a particular brand of politics as of the essence of the gospel. When individuals from other countries and cultures, with different political convictions, come to America, they are disenfranchised because the church has created unnecessary barriers to evangelism. Indeed, there is an unofficial color bar which runs through American church life, particularly as it relates to whites and African-Americans. This has roots deep in the history of the white churches' record on slavery and more than a little to do with current economic and class divisions, and is not helped by the fact that most white evangelicals are identified as Republicans, while most African-Americans are Democrats. Bluntly put, if I have to buy your political manifesto in order to buy your gospel, then your church is indulging in a dangerous confusion of categories and excluding individuals and groups from its congregation. They are excluded on grounds other than that of simply being outside of Christ. A gospel that is too American in this sense is no gospel at all.

This is where the work of Edward Said becomes something with which Christians should familiarize themselves. Said, a Palestinian intellectual who taught at the University of Columbia in New York for most of his career, was a controversial figure, not least for his articulation of the Palestinian cause in the United States. His scholarly contributions to literary theory and to classical music are noteworthy. It is, however, his insistence on the need for engaged intellectuals that is perhaps his greatest legacy to the wider world and one which the evangelical project of Carl Henry needs to hear.

SPEAKING THE TRUTH TO POWER

Said, a dazzlingly brilliant and eclectic thinker, was deeply influenced by the work of, among others, Antonio Gramsci, the Italian Marxist and fountainhead of much "New Left" thinking, Michel Foucault, the French post-structuralist, and Frantz Fanon, the French-Algerian theorist of decolonization.[8] From these he learned both the ways in which established power uses all aspects of wider culture in order to extend its own project of control and manipulation, and the need therefore to be critical of the culture in which one lives lest one be unwittingly co-opted into its wider agenda. His most famous articulation, perhaps overstatement, of this thesis was in his book *Orientalism*. Here he argued that "the Orient" was a construct of Western ideology and thus part of the mechanism of Western imperial power.[9] Then, in his more nuanced work *Culture and Imperialism*, he studied Western literature with a view to demonstrating how even authors such as Jane Austen wrote literature which both reflected the social and political

---

[8] A good, accessible introduction to Said's thinking is that by Shelley Walia, *Edward Said and the Writing of History* (London: Totem, 2001); see also David Barsamian, *Culture and Resistance: Conversations with Edward W. Said* (Cambridge: South End Press); Gauri Wiswanathan, *Power, Politics and Culture: Interviews with Edward Said* (New York: Vintage, 2001). His autobiography (to age 21) is also of interest to understanding his thought: *Out of Place* (New York: Vintage, 1999).

[9] London: Penguin, 1978.

ambitions of the nascent British Empire and therefore helped to naturalize such ideas so as to lift them above criticism.[10]

Unlike Foucault, however, there is an underlying optimism in Said's work. This is probably drawn both from his own experience of political struggle and his reading of Fanon. Said is not simply mesmerized by power as if by some unavoidable, unopposable absolute; instead, he considers that resistance to power is both possible and desirable, nay, imperative.[11] And this is where the engaged intellectual has his or her role to play: intellectuals are not to allow themselves to be co-opted into the wider project of the imperialist establishment. They have no choice but to work within it. Yet they can offer dissenting, critical voices which offer alternative narratives and possibilities of resistance to dominant powers. They are to learn to understand the way in which the media, scholarly guilds, indeed, all cultural institutions can be used to make the status quo appear as an absolute and all alternatives as mediocre. The engaged intellectual is "to speak the truth to power," to stand against the popular tide and to offer prophetic criticism of the abuse of power, no matter how "natural" that abuse may have been made to appear by the media or by the political and cultural traditions to which we may belong.[12]

Said identifies two aspects of modernity/postmodernity that are particularly lethal to this critical project. The first is the cult of specialization whereby those who speak outside of the sphere of competence for which they have the culturally approved credentials are regarded as illegitimately crossing boundaries. As we British would say, they are speaking out of their hats. The example which Said uses on occasion is that of left-wing American social critic, Noam Chomsky. Chomsky has

---

[10] London: Vintage, 1993.

[11] See his essay, "Foucault and the Imagination of Power," in *Reflections on Exile and Other Essays* (Cambridge: Harvard University Press, 2002), pp. 239–45.

[12] Said's view of the role of intellectuals, indebted as it is to figures such as Gramsci, Mary McCarthy, and Noam Chomsky, is most clearly articulated in his Reith Lectures, published as *Representations of the Intellectual* (London: Vintage, 1994).

made significant, if highly controversial and hotly contested, contributions to the field of theoretical linguistics. It is this area where he has formal academic qualifications, and his work is taken very seriously by the scholarly establishment. He has also made major contributions to understanding how propaganda functions, how the West has frequently played a duplicitous game with regard to human rights abuses and geopolitical issues. Yet in this area he has no formal qualifications—his work is often denigrated. This is not by virtue of it being intrinsically wrong or bad, but on the basis that he has no formal academic qualifications which would entitle him to speak to these matters. In other words, Said would say that the culture of academic specialization is being used by a political establishment to marginalize a dissenting voice. The academic culture effectively colludes in extending the power of the politicians by making illegitimate the contributions of those who do not possess the right membership card.

The second aspect of modernity/postmodernity which Said sees as lethal to the idea of the engaged intellectual is the fragmented and disengaged attitude fostered by the various forms of relativism. These present themselves as the vanguard of trendiness in the postmodern world.

Not for Said the simplistic metanarratival announcement of the "death of metanarratives." As with others on the Left, Said is both appreciative of the truly critical impulse which is to be found in aspects of such approaches but also deeply suspicious of the verbal Gnosticism and ultimate trivial sterility which has marked so much of this trajectory. In *Culture and Imperialism*, Said gives passionate expression to this sentiment:

> As for intellectuals whose charge includes values and principles—literary, philosophical, historical specialists— the American university, with its munificence, Utopian sanctuary, and remarkable diversity, has defanged them. Jargons of an almost unimaginable rebarbativeness dominate their styles. Cults like post-modernism, discourse analysis, New Historicism, deconstruction, neo-pragmatism transport them into the country of the blue. An astonishing sense of

weightlessness with regard to the gravity of history and individual responsibility fritters away attention to public matters and to public discourse.[13]

Said then lists racism, poverty, the environment, and disease as topics which receive less and less serious attention. The trivialization of intellectual pursuits is thus seen as part of the overall program of exalting Western society. Those who spend their time studying and lecturing on soap operas, cyberdating, and the Simpsons, without any reflective understanding of how these studies are themselves the wider political agenda, they are in danger of allowing the cultural relativism that is so loved by Western consumer society that it destroys their capacity for criticism and to co-opt them into the project of ignoring the things that really matter. The intellectual is not there just to go along with the dominant ideological patterns; he or she is there to offer criticism of those patterns to the extent that that is possible.[14]

What Can the Jerusalem of Henry Learn From the Athens of Said?

The lessons for evangelicals from Said are profound. Speaking personally, of all the non-Christian authors I have read, Said is the greatest influence on my own thinking. I believe that his insights speak quite clearly to weaknesses which have emerged in Henry's vision for the new evangelicalism. Indeed, his voice is one which evangelicals can hear with profit (and, given his graceful style, with pleasure too).

First, Said's notion of an engaged intellectual is very close to Henry's call for evangelicals to be culturally and politically engaged. It is, of course, true that no one can stand outside of culture; everyone exists in a particular time and place and is shaped by their environment. What Henry failed to anticipate

---

[13] *Culture and Imperialism*, pp. 366–67.

[14] This trivialization of intellectual pursuits in the wake of postmodernism has been noted by Terry Eagleton in *After Theory* (London: Penguin, 2003).

in 1948 was the way in which the evangelical project would become part and parcel of the American project. He did not see how it would so identify with various American causes in a highly polarized political environment, that, to many outsiders anyway, evangelicalism would become identified with certain political positions and self-criticism in the evangelical community would be effectively non-existent. This is as true of the political right as of the political left in evangelical circles. The left are very quick to grab hold of culturally trendy—dare one say safe?—causes, such as racism and sexual egalitarianism. But less popular concerns, such as Third World Debt, the Palestinian question, the environment, and AIDS/famine in sub-Saharan Africa, are of little importance in the religious politics of the evangelical left, just as they are of little interest to the secular left.[15] To those who hold to the Pauline teaching on sin, there would appear to be a horrible Pelagianism at work in such easy cultural accommodation. Said's notion of the engaged intellectual as one who sees the collusive nature of culture and power is one which anti-Pelagians should understand and appreciate. The role of engaged intellectuals, the modern-day prophets, begins with root and branch criticism of the culture to which they themselves belong. We need theologians and church leaders who are prepared to look at evangelicalism and see how and where this is being co-opted and corrupted by the agenda and priorities of the wider world. For my part, I would suggest that in the West the enemy at the moment is consumerism, reinforced by the old mythology of Western superiority. These foes are deadlier in many ways than the Red menace if only because they are that much more insidious and seductive. The internal enemies, those which insinuate themselves within our own ways of life, are always harder to spot and more difficult

---

[15] This is, of course, a very broad statement about the contours of general evangelical concerns. It is true that there are a growing number of exceptions: for example, the work by Gary Burge of Wheaton College, on the Palestinian question; the various writings of figures as diverse as Ron Sider and Os Guinness; magazines such as *Sojourners* and *Books and Culture*; and Joni Eareckson Tada's organization, *Joni and Friends*.

to defeat. The prophetic voice *must* speak to this in the coming years if the church is not to become a religious form of wholly secular substance. Henry was very careful not to make his call for political engagement a partisan appeal. Given the current polarization, it would seem that evangelicals need to heed the cultural criticism of a Said if they are to avoid a simplistic and idolatrous identification of Christianity with a particular political project, whether of the right or of the left.

Second, the cult of specialization needs to be resisted. I must be careful here: it is not wrong for Christians to aim to be as good as they can be in their chosen fields, and that applies to theological studies as much as to anything else. Specialization is acceptable, indeed, in many cases desirable. The *culture* of specialization, however, must not be allowed to render any particular group immune by default from criticism by any other group. That creates a context for the abuse of power, through the disempowerment of those who do not possess the right membership card to a particular guild, not because what they say is intrinsically wrong. Henry's appeal for Christians to obtain the appropriate educational qualifications and to be involved at the highest level in scholarly discussion was right and proper and necessary. To achieve this, evangelicals needed to negotiate with the non-evangelical academy as it set the terms and determined the frameworks for debate. At times, though, this negotiation has come to look more like capitulation. One aspect of this is the way in which specialization and disciplinary fragmentation has led to the erection of walls between scholarly guilds. An example of this can be the way synoptic scholars and systematicians feel unable to comment outside of their own fields and indeed resent any attempt by others to intrude on their own territory from outside. How this is to be overcome is not immediately obvious to me as I write. I am confident though that this is not simply a technical problem to be solved by training and expertise. It is also a deeper, cultural problem, and the solution will involve changes in attitude. It will also involve changes in vocabulary, since the generation of pretentious and opaque verbiage in many areas of specialization is surely as much a function of trying to reinforce the mystique of specialization as of the need to express oneself clearly and precisely in a technical context. If it is the latter which is the intention, someone needs to inform our hermeneutical brethren, preferably in words of just one or two syllables, that this is certainly not what is actually being achieved. Specialization which assumes to itself an invulnerability to criticism from outside is specialization which has made itself, and the power it wields, unaccountable to no one but those it chooses.

Finally, Said's warnings about the deleterious effects of the trivializing and absolute relativizing power of various strands of postmodernism need to be grasped. New evangelicalism in America has grabbed hold of such strands with a vengeance, and some good has come from this, for example: a serious desire for engagement with popular culture; also an awareness that the past—even the writing of the past—is in many ways problematic; and an apparent sensitivity to our own cultural situatedness and the need to respect other cultures. But if Said's comments on the way such relativist philosophies ultimately collude with wider cultural trends, either by shrinking all issues down to the same trivial moral level or by removing any basis for social criticism are true, then we need to ask whether trendy evangelical postmodernism is anything more than a surreptitious and devastating attempt to "defang," to use Said's term, the gospel of its critical power. Is Christian postmodern relativism simply another example of how evangelicalism has mortgaged its soul to Western consumerism and now pays uncritical—and often unwitting—homage to the idol of Western values?[16] Again, the answer to the problem

---

[16] I am also persuaded by the arguments of Frederic Jameson, Perry Anderson, and Terry Eagleton (and articulated in a Christian context by individuals such as Stanley Hauerwas) that there is a connection between postmodern relativist epistemologies and consumerism. If this is the case, then the rise of postmodern evangelical thinking, the entrepreneurial culture of American evangelicalism, and the apparent ideological chaos of an organ such as *Christianity Today*, which I mentioned above, can be seen as part and parcel of one and the same agenda—a classic, Saidian connection of ideological, institutional, cultural, and economic

is not easy. An awareness, however, that postmodernism, in its crude, popular forms, may be part of the problem rather than part of the solution, will mark a starting point for further critical reflection on how it functions as an ideology in the contemporary Christian world and beyond.

Strange bedfellows indeed. One was the all-American Christian journalist with a vision for evangelicalism that shaped a generation, the other the secular Palestinian intellectual and exile whose writings on politics and culture consistently challenged the ruling consensus and presented the claims of the marginalized to an indifferent or hostile world. Neither man, I am sure, would appreciate the company of the other. Yet Henry's ambitious project clearly needs the critical edge of a Said if it is to be faithful to its task of true engagement rather than mere cultural collusion. Henry spoke of the uneasy conscience of fundamentalism. Yet the various sects of modern American evangelicalism, while very angry with just about everybody else, too often seem very comfortable and at ease with themselves. Indeed, they seem to have the easy consciences of those Pelagians who see the enemy everywhere except in their own hearts. And yet in this context there seem no creeds better designed to maintain this easiness of the modern evangelical conscience than those which rejoice uncritically in the Western way, whether right of left; or which delight in differences and offer no satisfactory basis for discerning the good from the bad, the vitally important from the utterly trivial; or which fail to see the way in which evangelicalism, often at the very point where it smugly thinks of itself as most engaged and culturally savvy, is too often the unwitting and uncritical ally of larger political and cultural agendas which have nothing to do with biblical Christianity. At this hour, we do not need yet another trendy pundit to salve consciences through superficial cultural commentary involving Christian approaches to Britney Spears, dental floss, or beer commercials. Such characters are

---

power. On the whole, Christian postmodern pundits have not taken with sufficient seriousness the material conditions in which the various philosophies routinely categorized as "postmodern" occur.

next to useless in the struggles which Christianity faces at this time. Instead we need Christian Saids who will not waste time on junk but rather will dare to speak the truth to power in all circumstances and however uneasy it might make our consciences.

1.3

THE BANALITY OF EVIL: FROM EICHMANN TO THE iPOD GENERATION

When I accepted the invitation to speak here tonight, the original title which I was given was, "Who is capable of evil?" I decided fairly quickly to change this because, as my PA said to me, once I had provided the single word answer "Everyone," there would be very little left to say. Further, I am a historian, not a philosopher or a politician or a theologian; thus, I am not really qualified to address questions of evil in any deep or abstract or theoretical sense; instead, what I do is examine all questions historically, through the lens of the rough and ready particulars of history; thus, tonight I want to address the original question, "Who is capable of evil?" by looking at a specific manifestation of historic evil, that of the Final Solution, and of a central figure in that tragedy, Adolf Eichmann.

First, however, it will be useful to spend a few moments reflecting on the image of evil in our culture. The image of evil in culture, whether high or low (if those terms are at all meaningful), indicates very clearly the fact that we, as human beings, find it to be fascinating. Evil characters in plays, books, and movies are often portrayed as strangely attractive through their cool sophistication and intellectual superiority to so many of their opponents. Thus, we have Shakespeare's Iago and Macbeth and Richard III; we have Professor Moriarty, the criminal genius of the Sherlock Holmes novels; Hannibal Lecter, the terrifying yet sophisticated cannibal and serial killer; the Green Goblin and Dr Octopus, the mortal foes of Spiderman; Lex Luthor, Superman's nemesis; and any number of James Bond's opponents, from Dr No through Goldfinger down to LeChiffre. Many of these characters are, arguably, just as interesting, if not really more interesting than their somewhat purer opponents. And there are subtle ways in which this fascination with the sophistication of evil manifests itself. For example, American movies and television programs contain a highly disproportionate number of screen villains who have English accents. Indeed, in any whodunnit where one of the characters is English, it is relatively easy to guess who committed the murder from the moment said character opens his or her mouth. In a recent series of 24, even the Russian villain spoke with an impeccable English accent. The accent betrays the moral depravity, the *sophisticated* moral depravity, that lurks beneath the superficially polite façade.

These cultural phenomena allow us to draw two conclusions. First, evil is fascinating. That's why it sells so well as a commodity in the entertainment marketplace. To put it bluntly, evil is on the whole much more interesting and entertaining than its opposite; it is virtually a commodity which, and, when added to other products, makes them much more marketable. What is it that makes *Lord of the Rings* so interesting? It is the evil and the conflict that evil brings with it. Or take the *Divine Comedy* of Dante Alighieri, with its three parts, *Hell*, *Purgatory*, and *Paradise*. I cannot quote chapter and verse, but if I were a betting man I would put my money on the fact that the most widely read of the three sections would be *Hell*, with *Purgatory* a poor second, and *Paradise* a very distant third. Why do I say this? Simply because evil, and the pain and suffering it generates, is more interesting to read about than the kind of idyllic bliss one finds in *Paradise*. Eternal bliss might truly be wonderful; the image of angels sitting on clouds and playing harps has its attractions; but it is far more boring as a spectator sport than the spectacular fireworks and terrifying sights of the *Inferno*.

The second conclusion is that evil is generally conceived of by us as being sophisticated and exceptional. Of course, there are various myths about evil which, on the surface, seem to run counter to this thesis, for example, the common assumption, often reinforced by media reports, that serial killers keep themselves to themselves, are good neighbors, and have all the appearance of being ordinary. Such may sometimes be the case in real life; but in the way that such are presented in cultural artifacts such as novels and movies, this normality is usually presented as a cleverly constructed screen which hides the malignant and sophisticated evil which lurks beneath the surface of suburban respectability. We seem to need evil to be clever and exceptional. Why is this? I would suggest that, at a simple level and in connection to my earlier point, sophisticated evil makes better copy, being far more fascinating and entertaining. But I would also suggest that, perhaps, making evil exceptional in this way allows us to distance ourselves from what is being depicted. As the news media can play up the outward normality of serial killers to scare us (perhaps to thrill us? Is the American news media not simply one more form of entertainment) by making us think that anyone, even nice Mr Jones on the corner, could be the next Boston Strangler, so the portrayal of evil as exceptional in novels and movies entertains us yet simultaneously allows us to distance ourselves from it. And the news media are quite capable of playing this game when it suits them as well. The portrayal of enemy leaders, whether Russians in the Cold War or Iraqis in more recent days, allows us to assume that the ordinary rules which apply to us do not apply to them, because they are sophisticated evil incarnate.

To pull these thoughts together: it seems to me to be indisputable that evil fascinates us; and that the normative portrayal of evil in plays and novels and movies indicates that we are particularly fascinated by evil as a clever, sophisticated thing, something which we can immediately distance ourselves from on the grounds that it is exceptional, something that is other than ourselves; but also something which, by virtue of its sophistication, fascinates and interests us yet more.

So much for the cultural portrayal of evil. Of course, this is all mythology. By *mythology*, of course, I do not mean that these portraits of evil have no extra-textual referentiality, nothing to which they correspond in the real world. What I mean is that they are mythological in the way they present reality in a particular way, to achieve certain ends or create certain realities: to entertain us; to justify certain social conventions; to confirm our opinion that evil is something involving other, exceptional people and not ourselves, etc.

Given this, I now want to turn our attention to the work from which I have drawn part of the title of this lecture: Hannah Arendt's account (originally written as a series of articles for *The New Yorker*) of the trial of Nazi war criminal, Adolf Eichmann, for war crimes before a Jerusalem court in 1962. Eichmann had been a member of the SS and a man responsible for significant parts of the administration of the Final Solution. He had attended the notorious Wannsee Conference, where the extermination of the Jews had been formulated as a specific Nazi policy. He had helped develop the logistics of genocide. Then, after the war, he had fled Germany in 1950 and lived in Argentina until his kidnapping by Israeli agents in 1960. Taken back to Israel, he had faced trial in Jerusalem, sitting for his own protection in a glass box throughout the court proceedings; he had been found guilty; and then he had been executed. Hannah Arendt, a leading woman philosopher, a German, and a Jew, had reported on the trial and the end product was a book not simply of journalistic reportage but also of philosophical and social criticism of totalitarianism, of genocide, and of the men and women who implement the same.[1]

Arendt's book was very controversial at the time, but holds numerous points of interest when it comes to trying

---

[1] The edition I have used for this lecture is Hannah Arendt, *Eichmann in Jerusalem: A Report on the Banality of Evil* (London: Penguin, 1977).

to understand the nature of evil. For a start, the Holocaust is so vast, both in terms of the depth, intentionality, and thoroughness of its evil, and in terms of the complexity, technological and otherwise, of its execution. It is, perhaps, the supreme example of conscious human evil on all levels, from the moral to the technical; and with Eichmann as one of the players, one might expect that he would represent in some microcosmic way these attributes of the greater whole—an ideologically driven, brilliantly evil genius determined upon greater and greater acts of wickedness. Yet, in fact, the picture painted by Arendt is decidedly more complex and subversive of many of the clichés of pop culture views of evil.

What most struck Arendt about Eichmann was not that he was an evil genius of exceptional immoral talent; rather, it was his utter ordinariness. Frankly, he came across as dull and thoughtless. His problem, she observed, was not a surfeit of ideology; it was a deficit of thought. He had a complete inability to grasp the extent of his crimes, to sympathize with his victims, or to understand that he was responsible in any way for the mass murders which he helped to facilitate. He could not even grasp why he had not advanced further up the Nazi hierarchy than he had in fact done. In other words, Eichmann seemed to Arendt to be a fairly typical specimen of humanity.

Such a view was highly offensive to many. Some interpreted Arendt as excusing Eichmann on the grounds that the category she used to explain him—banality, his very unexceptionally boring persona—seemed too normal and too remote from the moral categories necessary to evaluate and condemn a man involved in such crimes. Others saw the alleged ordinariness of Eichmann as humanizing him in a way that made him into a more sympathetic figure. Finally, Arendt (herself Jewish) pointed out the complicity of numerous Jewish figures and organizations in implementing the Final Solution. There was the tragic figure of Dr Kastner, a leading figure in the Budapest Jewish community, who negotiated with Eichmann and obtained safety for a few thousand Jews who were allowed to emigrate in exchange for guaranteeing the peaceful compliance of hundreds of thousands with the Nazis in a manner which guaranteed their own deaths. And everywhere Arendt's narrative is haunted by the question: how could a comparatively small number of Nazi functionaries have dispatched so many Jews to the gas chambers? Why did not more fight back? For this, Arendt found herself attacked as a self-hating Jew.

Setting aside such heartbreaking questions, I want to focus on two issues which emerge from Arendt's portrayal of Eichmann and which, I believe, are most significant for reflecting on the nature of evil and the human capacity for it. These are the role of clichés and the role of technology. Both played a significant role in the Holocaust in general and in the role of Eichmann in particular; both played to his utter thoughtlessness and banality; and both place demands upon us.

THE POWER OF CLICHÉ

One thing which Arendt noted about Eichmann was his inability to speak in anything other than the official jargon of the Nazi regime and of the bureaucracy he served, and in self-invented clichés which, we might say, put his own anodyne, if not positive, spin on all events. Thus, he was able to package the horrors of the Final Solution, and of his central role within it, in language which avoided entirely the deep moral questions which such complicity in mass murder should have raised. In a telling moment while imprisoned in Jerusalem, he was given a copy of Nabokov's *Lolita* to read by his young prison guard; he returned it two days later, describing it as "Quite an unwholesome book."[2] So mass murder becomes a mere function of bureaucracy and consequently provokes no feelings in Eichmann of moral outrage; while a sexually explicit classic of twentieth-century literature earns his horror and scorn.

Arendt's conclusion on this point runs as follows:

The longer one listened to him, the more obvious it became that his inability to speak was closely connected to an inability

---

[2] Arendt, 49.

to think, namely to think from the standpoint of somebody else. No communication was possible with him, not because he lied but because he was surrounded by the most reliable of all safeguards against the words and the presence of others, and hence against reality as such.[3]

Cliches, then, are the enemy not simply of clear communication but also of thoughtful social and moral action. They allowed Eichmann to inhabit a world which simply did not have to address the needs or the feelings of others, or his own wider moral and social responsibilities. Arendt gives numerous examples which came up at the trial, some comic, some tragic.[4] What they all indicate is Eichmann's complete inability to think.

. How is that relevant to us? Well, to return to my original question: who is capable of evil? I answered, "Everyone"; and while I would defend that as true, it is a somewhat unsatisfactory answer from a historical point of view. It is rather like asking the question as to why the Twin Towers collapsed on September 11, 2001 and answering "Gravity." A true answer, but a wholly inadequate one as far as making sense of the particular outrage under consideration. So, why did Eichmann commit evil? In part because he lost whatever ability he might ever have had for thoughtful action through his uncritical absorption and use of the clichéd world which he had come to inhabit. And we need to make sure that we, as individuals and as a society, resist the temptation to become subject to the same.

We live in a democracy, and democracy, of course, depends for its good health upon a healthy and free exchange of nuanced ideas. Yet it also places distinct limits on nuance: however complicated the various issues—economic, moral, and social—of today may be, when you step into the voting booth you can only vote for one party; thus, all but the most benighted party hack is likely to have to trade off agreements and disagreements with a party platform as they tick the

---

[3] Ibid.
[4] Arendt, 48–53.

relevant box. Yet as television and the internet increasingly reduce political debate to the level of sound bites, image, and aesthetics, making political decisions virtually a matter of taste rather than argument, the language of public discourse becomes increasingly clichéd in a manner which hamstrings our ability to speak, thus to think, and thus to act. The reduction, say, of the abortion debate to the bumper sticker slogans "Pro-life" and "Pro-choice" is, for example, inimical to thoughtful engagement with the issue. A complex issue has become encapsulated in a soundbite; and the use of the first label by those who plant bombs in clinics, and the second by those who campaign to stop anti-abortionists from having a public platform, speaks volumes about the way the clichés have taken on a life of their own and seriously impaired the ability of those who use them to make choices consistent even with their own stated morality.

Now, language is something public and communal, not the product of isolated individuals; and as such it is always vulnerable to being clichéd, to being taken for granted, and used by us in a way that excuses us from having to think for ourselves. Perhaps nowhere is this more in evidence today on the far wing of the so-called "Religious Right" where terms such as "liberal" and "social welfare" have become so self-evidently pejorative that it is well-nigh impossible to engage in intelligent debate about what they actually represent in real terms. And the secular left indulges in the same abuse of language: anyone of traditional religious sympathies is a fundamentalist, again precluding intelligent debate.

And the problem does not end with the killing of debate; the power of clichés extends, as with Eichmann, to moral abdication of personal responsibility. Once I have labeled someone a *fundamentalist* or a *liberal*, I no longer have the obligation to deal with them as one human being to another; their humanity has been eclipsed by the reification of some view they hold which now gives me an exhaustive, and subhuman, account of who they are. I could go on—the supplanting of the categories of moral responsibility with the idiom of addiction again shows the power of cliché to strip us of our humanity. No longer do I waste money on buying classic rock albums from the seventies—now I am addicted to shopping; no longer do I duplicitously cheat on my wife— rather, I am suffering from the illness of sex addiction. Further, the language of go-getting American optimism linked to any number of technological innovations, and, more crucially, the business world surrounding them, renders thoughtful criticism of Information Technology at best redundant, at worst the activity of Luddite curmudgeons.

Yet there is more. In Nazi Germany, the clichéd language of officialdom was part and parcel of a self-referential, self-justifying system of oppression. While it was undoubtedly true that Eichmann had a choice—other SS men refused their murderous tasks and were simply seconded to other duties—there can be little doubt that the language of Nazi bureaucracy was seductive to many, especially those who bought so deeply into the system that they lost their ability to think for themselves. The same applies today, as anyone who has ever had to deal with a representative of a government agency or an insurance company will no doubt be able to confirm. Bureaucracy creates its own official language which serves to justify both its means and its ends.

In this context, I might add that I find myself in basic agreement with Terry Eagleton's critique of certain strands of contemporary thought which so emphasize the linguistic nature of reality that they effectively preclude any opportunity of mounting a significant challenge to the status quo. In such schemes, language is no longer a means of communication; it is rather a prison house which determines the very nature and limits of reality itself. Protest is impossible because the tools of protest are themselves internalized as soon as they are produced. Moreover, universities and colleges, the very places where critical thought should be encouraged and cultivated, have fallen prey to their own clichés of "postmodernism" and "professionalism," with all the pragmatism that they bring in their wake. The radical fragmentation of academic disciplines, with the concomitant development of the rebarbative and arcane language which specialization brings in its wake, has served to render higher education not a context for developing independent thinking but for fostering a trivialization of values, where PhDs on hotel management and on body piercing at the Jersey shore have as much legitimacy as those dealing with what would once have been considered the great questions of life: eternal salvation or class struggle or world poverty or nuclear war.

So, to conclude this section, the banality of Eichmann is surely a warning from history to us all: clichés of language, of politics, of bureaucracy have a power which we underestimate at our peril; and yet we live in a world which, through the dominance of televisual media and sound bite politics, makes it increasingly difficult to think in anything but clichés. And that has significant implications for how we think, or do not think, and how we consequently act.

THE POWER OF TECHNOLOGY
The second striking aspect of Eichmann is the role that technique and technology played in his crimes, and in his own understanding of them. There is a very real and very chilling sense in which Eichmann regarded himself simply as a logistics man. This is, of course, intimately connected to the clichés into which he bought concerning his task. He was the facilitator, the man who made things happen, who brought to pass the orders of his superiors. In practice, this meant that he was the guy who had to make sure the trains ran on time with the right people on board, and that they arrived at the right place. That the right people were Jews and gypsies, and that the right place was Auschwitz may strike terror in our hearts; but to him it was just a job.[5]

With the one exception of slapping a Jewish official in the face (an incident for which Eichmann apparently apologized), there is no evidence that he was personally sadistic or brutal towards his victims at all. He is, therefore, a good, albeit extreme, example of the way in which technology can be

---

[5] See, for example, Arendt, 140, dealing with the deportations from Budapest.

used by human beings to distance themselves from the various consequences of their actions and of the societies to which they belong. We are all no doubt familiar with this in terms of more commonplace examples. Thus, I have vegetarian friends who tell me that if I had to kill cows and pigs and sheep myself, I would quickly turn vegetarian. I imagine I could probably get used to the role of butcher, but the point is well-made: I would, at least, have a very different attitude to the meat I ate if I had to slaughter it myself. Technology alienates me from the meat industry, an alienation for which I am quite grateful every time I tuck into a nice juicy steak.

In the context of Eichmann's role in the Final Solution, we see how the world of clichés in which he lived combined with technology to insulate him from the obvious moral issues. He killed no one; rather, he simply obeyed orders. He inflicted pain on no one; he simply made sure the trains ran on time and that the commandants at the various death camps were ready to receive the deported Jews which he sent their way. He was simply a very *efficient* worker, a small cog within a larger impersonal machine that was simply getting a particular job done. He felt no responsibility for the racist ideology underlying the Final Solution. Indeed, he was an admirer of Theodore Herzl, the founder of Zionism; and he even had a Jewish mistress in Vienna, quite simply the most heinous crime which an SS office could commit. And he felt no responsibility for the mass executions in the gas chambers of Auschwitz. He gassed no one. He was simple the middle man, the facilitator.

Again, how does this connect to us? Well, it would be silly to engage in the argument that we are all complicit in something akin to the Final Solution. Thankfully that is not the case: there are no camps of systematic, mass human extermination of which I am aware in the United States. Yet we do live in a world where technology has displaced virtue; or, perhaps better still, technology has become virtue. There is a strong current in contemporary culture which seems to see problems of personal morality as things to be addressed with technological answers. Take a trivial example: antisocial cellphone use in theaters. In order to solve this problem, some theaters have been looking at the possibility of installing technology which will block cellphone reception during performance times. The problem would seem to be a moral one: the selfishness of certain members of the audience; the solution is a technological one—it seeks to address the issue without tackling the question of the moral responsibility of the audience. There are plenty of other examples: the perennial calls for car engines to be fitted with damping devices to stop drivers breaking the speed limit; the development of breath-test devices to stop cars being started by drivers over the legal blood-alcohol levels. My point, of course, is not that such developments are necessarily bad or unhelpful or wrong; but rather that they are interesting as responses because of what they do not address. They offer technological solutions to moral problems which actually arise through the inappropriate behavior of individuals. They indicate the existence of a culture where technology is effectively ascribed moral powers and competences in and of itself. And this technological pragmatism is dangerous precisely because, as with clichés, it allows us to abdicate our moral responsibilities. When we come to believe that moral problems can have technological solutions, then we reduce morality itself to a matter of pure pragmatics—mere convenience and technique.

In fact, of course, the language frequently applied to science and technology has itself often become a cliché, and this combination is particularly potent. Again, the Eichmann trial provided a first-class example of this. Eichmann's lawyer, Dr Servatius, was a tax and business legal specialist from Cologne. He was an ordinary German who had never even joined the Nazi party. Yet in his closing statement to the court, he declared his client innocent of "the collection of skeletons, sterilizations, killings by gas, and *similar medical matters.*" Arendt continues:

> Judge Halevi interrupted him: "Dr Servatius, I assume you made a slip of the tongue when you said that killing by gas was

a medical matter." To which Servatius replied: "It was indeed a medical matter, since it was prepared by physicians; it was a matter of killing, and killing too is a medical matter."[6]

Servatius was to use the same cliché, "medical matter," to refer to the conscious act of mass murder on at least one other occasion in the court documents. Technology meets cliché; and mass murder and moral responsibility are effectively erased with a mere flourish of a linguistic wand.

Some so-called postmodern pundits, of course, might well dismiss this concern by making a great play of the crisis in confidence in science. Critiquing that viewpoint would be a lecture in itself, but suffice it to say here that I do not see much, if any, evidence of this crisis outside of the lecture theaters of said pundits. At a popular cultural level, it seems self-evident that the appetite among the public for more technology, and for the latest models of everything, from computers to washing machines, is insatiable; and Richard Dawkins's book, *The God Delusion*, has sold in quantities of which most of the prophets of the death of science can only dream. Indeed, you can write as many books as you want about the collapse of science, but the likelihood is you will do it on a state-of-the-art computer powered by electricity provided by a state-of-the-art power station.

Science and technology are here to stay as dominant cultural forces; and that is good. I like new computers; I like flush toilets; I like antibiotics; I like being able to fly back to the UK and drink decent beer once in a while. But it is imperative that we are aware of the dangers of allowing technology to create a world in which we are able to abdicate moral responsibility. When bureaucracy and technology create giant and apparently impersonal systems, then it becomes possible for each of the individual people involved in the system to ignore their responsibility for the consequences of that system. Of such was the Holocaust; and in our increasingly bureaucratized and technologized society, the potential for such abdication is surely that much greater.

---

[6] Arendt, 69.

SOME CHRISTIAN OBSERVATIONS

So far, I have offered an account of Arendt's portrait of Eichmann relative to the implementation of the Holocaust. While I speak from a self-consciously Christian perspective, little if anything that I have said so far is explicitly Christian in content. I wish now in this final section to offer some observations where my Christian commitments are perhaps more obvious. I do so with two specific intentions in mind. First, I want to make the case that Christianity offers a framework within which the lessons of Eichmann can be appropriated and reinforced; and, secondly, in so doing I want at least to sow seeds in your minds that the popular media image of Christianity as a necessarily reactionary, right-wing, and socially irresponsible movement may not be all that it seems. I would be the first to admit that the history of the church and of many individual Christians is less than stellar; but I want to make the case that the Christian faith offers intellectual resources which do give a frame of reference for learning from the Holocaust.

First, basic to Arendt's analysis of Eichmann is her observation that he was incapable of seeing anything from the point of view of his victims. This was in part due to the absorption of the very clever language-world of the SS Heinrich Himmler, the Reichsfuhrer SS and the man in ultimate charge of the Final Solution was always careful not to deny the horrific nature of the task in which his men were involved; but rather than saying "Isn't the slaughter of Jews horrific?" he created a culture where the question would be posed as "Isn't what we have to endure for the greater good of the Reich horrific?" Thus, the suffering impacts the perpetrator, not the victim. And Eichmann's own testimony patterns this: his account of seeing Jews gassed and shot focuses on the horror he feels, not the terrible fate of the Jews themselves.

What makes this possible? The ability of the SS officers to separate themselves from their victims, and, underlying this, a denial of the common humanity of both. The possibility of the Final Solution was predicated on the abolition of common human nature. That is in part why ordinary people committed such terrible outrages: years of anti-Semitic propaganda had prepared the ground that reduced the Jews to less than human in the eyes of others. A similar thing occurred in the Soviet Union, where again propaganda abolished common human nature and facilitated the gulags.

Dare I say it, but this abolition of human nature lies at the heart of much post-structuralist philosophy. The work of Foucault and Derrida, for all of its seductive sophistication, is targeted at the abolition of human nature. As such, it not only renders human beings impotent in the face of oppression, undercutting the possibility of resisting power; it also destroys any possibility of articulating human rights. Human rights are at best a more or less arbitrary social construct of no more than local interest; at worst, they are simply part of a Western conspiracy to impose Western values on the rest of the world as if they possessed transcendent reality. If human nature has no meaning, then human rights have no meaning either, and the safeguards against something like the Holocaust are dramatically weakened. The first step towards becoming like Eichmann is taken when, either through thoughtlessness or through ideological conviction, we come to deny the common humanity we all share. If, however, we understand that no man or woman is an island, that we are all part of the whole, that the suffering of the starving in Africa or the homeless on the streets of Philadelphia implicates me because I am human as they are human, then the need for me to take responsibility and to act is clear. And of such is the biblical teaching on the nature of humanity—made in the image of God, defined by the story of creation and fall.

Second, while Arendt never uses this terminology, it is clear that she saw Eichmann as being one who engaged in a form of idolatry. Now, let me be clear what I am saying here. *Idolatry*, as I use the term, does not have the crude meaning of bowing down in front of a carved image of a god and worshiping it. That is idolatry, but only in its most blatant form. Rather, I use the term here in a manner akin to the Marxist concept of the *fetish*. A fetish is something to which human beings ascribe a power which it does not possess in and of itself. Thus, many in Philadalphia make a fetish of the Eagles. The power of winning the superbowl is ascribed to them on an annual basis; and every year this ascription proves to be false. Eichmann appears to have made a fetish or an idol out of two things: first, the bureaucratic system within which he was involved was viewed by him as so absolute and all-encompassing that it could not be disobeyed. Qualms of conscience that appear to have occasionally bubbled up in his consciousness were quickly dismissed because his faith in the system allowed him to abdicate responsibility: he told himself that he was just a small cog in a giant machine, that his personal opinions must clearly be brought into line with those whom he respected and were superior to him in the system. And his second idol was the language he used: by talking a good game, by reminding himself and others that everyone was "pulling together for a greater cause," he appears to have invested these clichés with the power to absolve himself of any guilt or responsibility for his criminal actions. One could perhaps sum up these two idolatries by saying that Eichmann's ultimate crime was idolatry of self—whatever it was that he needed to have reality in his universe for him to be free of all responsibility, he would give it reality; he would make the laws he needed to make; and in so doing, he ceased to be human in any meaningful sense.

Christianity offers critical response to both of these idolatries. First, in its commitment to the idea that human beings are universally prone to idolatry, universally prone to ascribing godlike powers to that which is not God, it subjects all products of human culture to radical criticism. All systems are, at best, flawed. Christianity also emphasizes our accountability as individuals, not just as cogs within giant machines. No system, bureaucratic or otherwise, can be reified in such a way as to allow us to pass on our guilt to it. Human beings, human persons, are the units of accountability, not systems. And for all of the appropriate emphasis over recent decades upon structural wrongdoing, whether institutional racism or greed or whatever, Christianity should protest the extent to which even these often valid criticisms can be used to evade personal responsibility. Further, flawed systems cannot be simply replaced with unflawed systems; the fact that they are designed by and populated with human beings precludes at the outset that kind of constructed utopia.

Second, in its emphasis on a real world out there, Christianity stands in opposition to any notion that reality, physical or moral, can be merely a linguistic construct. To argue the latter is to make language into an idol, in much the way Eichmann appears to have done. Eichmann might even be the poster boy for certain contemporary views of language. He played his community's language game almost to perfection, imbibed Himmler's clichés, and threw in a few of his own to the point where he genuinely could not see the problem with sending millions of his fellow human beings to their death. Sure, he showed visible distress at his trial when individual accounts were given of SS brutality; but the problem was that he thought such individual acts of murder were *inhumane* and not *humane* as those meted out in the gas chambers of Auschwitz and Bergen-Belsen. He had so enclosed himself within the world of Nazi clichés that not even the rumblings of his conscience could find any coherent verbal expression. And such is the logical result of an approach to the world which loses track of the fact that there is a reality—physical and moral—beyond linguistic construction. In a world of competing, incommensurable narratives, the Ku Klux Klan or the neo-Nazis or even the Elvis impersonators can offer their view of reality and there is no way it can ultimately be challenged. But Christianity stands in opposition to this: the world is real; and men and women are held accountable to standards beyond their own immanent language, no matter how they try to insulate themselves from this greater reality. We are not human because of our ability to be those who make their own rules and adopt whatever view of reality appeals to us; rather we are human as we come to understand our common human nature and the limits that places upon us.

So, to return to where we started: is evil as glamorous and exciting and exceptional as the purveyors of pop culture might have us believe? Is it simultaneously something which is both thrillingly entertaining but also reassuringly different to ourselves? The answer I would give is the one that Arendt offered in her analysis of Eichmann. Evil is banal. It is commonplace. It is humdrum and everyday. Eichmann is an extreme example; but the terrifying thing about him—and about the countless other horrors that were recounted at his trial, from the mass shootings of civilians in the eastern territories to the collusion of high ranking Jewish officials in the murder of their own people—is the nagging suspicion that these people, these vile people, were in significant ways no different to ourselves. The honest reader is disturbed not by Eichmann's strangeness to ourselves, but by the questions his banal, evil life places at our own doorsteps. How would we have reacted? Would we have been heroes? Or would we have sought ways to look after number one? Would we have been more disturbed by the impact of murder on ourselves than upon the victims? If Arendt is right, if Eichmann's problem was not a surfeit of perverted ideology but a deficit of thought, then that is a most uncomfortable notion; and these questions become particularly haunting. The critical issue then becomes, how do we learn to think? I would suggest that Christianity, far from being an ideology which simply serves the political agenda of any given group in society, actually offers a probing, critical searchlight into the souls of us all, and gives us key tools for salutary critique of ourselves and of others.

1.4

IT AIN'T OVER TILL
THE FAT LADY SINGS[1]

Mark Noll is well known both within and without evangelicalism as an outstanding scholar, a gracious and thoughtful
commentator on religion and America, and one of the most
significant public religious intellectuals of the last decade.
Indeed, disagreeing with him is not something that one does
lightly; and I confess I am less than eager so to do. Yet reading
the recent book which he has coauthored with journalist,
Carolyn Nystrom, I find that I must register my dissent on a
number of key issues.

As one would expect from any book which carries Mark
Noll's name on its cover, the work is meticulously researched,
very clearly written, and exhibits a generosity of spirit that will
be disarming even to its critics, among whom it will be clear
I number myself. The insights it contains are also fascinating.
For example, as a foreigner on American soil, I found the
book extremely useful in outlining and explaining the history
of Catholic-Evangelical relations in US society. It is, after all,
puzzling to an outsider that as late as 1960, a presidential

---

[1] A Review of Mark Noll and Carolyn Nystrom, *Is the Reformation
Over?* (Grand Rapids: Eerdmans, 2005).

candidate's Catholicism was seen as an electoral liability, particularly with reference to the conservative Protestant sections of the electorate; and it is arguable that Kennedy won the election *despite* his religion and then only because he managed successfully to distance himself somewhat from it; yet in 2004 it was John F. Kerry's perceived failure to be a consistent Catholic on issues such as abortion and sanctity of life-related matters which was seen as the electoral problem, particularly with that same, conservative Protestant core. Much of the answer to this conundrum, of course, lies with Roe vs. Wade and the way in which the abortion debate in America has polarized society, politicized the judicial process, placed moral issues at the center of politics, and driven religious conservatives, Catholic and Protestant, into an unlikely alliance which 50 years ago would have seemed inconceivable. Now it seems (at least to an outsider) that much of the evangelical hopes, culturally and politically, hang on the decisions of Catholics such as Roberts and Scalia on the Supreme Court. Indeed, if, as this change perhaps implies, evangelicalism functions for some, or perhaps for many, of its adherents not so much as a statement about God but rather as an idiom for protesting the moral chaos in America, we can expect to see yet more rapprochement and maybe even significant numbers of conversions from evangelicalism to Rome, especially given the potential for clear moral leadership by the Catholic Church under the pontificate of Benedict XVI.

The story is, of course, more complex than just Roe vs. Wade, and, after an opening chapter which highlights the change in attitude of evangelicals to Rome, Noll and Nystrom proceed in the next two chapters to describe in more detail how the change took place, highlighting wider social and more narrowly ecclesiastical and institutional changes. This is followed by chapters on the various formal dialogues between mainstream Protestant denominations and Rome, on the Catholic *Catechism*, on the series of dialogues and documents known as *Evangelicals and Catholics Together* (ECT), on the various reactions, positive and negative, to ECT, and on the specific American situation relative to evangelical-Catholic relations. The conclusion borrows the title of the book "Is the Reformation Over?" and offers a generally—though not entirely—affirmative answer to that question. As a guide to the "state of the art" as regards Evangelical-Catholic relations, both in terms of history and wider context, the book is an invaluable must-read for all thoughtful Christians.

As I read the book, however, the words of a song by Rainbow (another seventies rock combo, I'm afraid) came repeatedly to mind: "I can't let you go, even though it's over!" There is indeed a sense in which this book demonstrates that the Reformation is over; but I would argue that this end to the Reformation has come about for many of the wrong reasons and represents not so much the final rapprochement between Catholicism and Protestantism but the problematic nature, if not crisis, of evangelical identity at the start of the twenty-first century. I'm afraid I for one can't let the Reformation go doctrinally, even though for many the curtain already appears to be coming down on the final scene.

The major problem with the book, and one which significantly skews some of the analysis, is the central place it accords to the relationship between Catholicism and evangelicalism. Thus, at the outset, we have an institutional church, with clearly defined authority structures, creeds, and an identifiable history—in other words, a self-conscious identity—being discussed in relation to a movement which lacks all of these things and is really only unified by a somewhat nebulous and ill-defined field of family resemblances—and family resemblances which have, over the years, become increasingly vague. This is at its most obvious, and acute, in the ECT discussions. In these, while both groups of participants were arguably self-appointed, the Catholics did at least stand as representatives of a church and knew for whom and for what they stood; whom exactly were the evangelicals representing? From their very inception, therefore, the ECT discussions were built upon an important category mistake: Catholics came to the table committed by church affiliation to a clear set of doctrinal principles; that commitment gave them a place to stand from which they could engage. The evangelicals had no such thing, no place to stand, nowhere from which to engage. This probably goes a long way to explaining the fact that, in terms of doctrinal agreement, the discussions appeared to achieve so much but actually did little more than demonstrate the "mere Christianity" perspective to which an eclectic, parachurch movement like evangelicalism inevitably tends; and thus they exposed the inability of such a movement to be truly distinctive when faced with a coherent, comprehensive, and self-conscious church body.

Take, for example, the touchstone issue of justification by grace through faith by the imputation of Christ's righteousness. In the account given here, the issue is all but laid to rest, and that on two grounds. First, the various ecumenical agreements are presented as indicating that there is no remaining substantial disagreement between Catholics and Protestants on the issue; and, second, the authors argue that few evangelicals still hold to the classic Protestant understanding of justification as being by the imputation of Christ's righteousness, and that by grace through faith.

Numerous lines of critique suggest themselves at this point. First, it is significant that, with the exception of the agreement between the Lutheran World Federation and the Catholics in 1999, none of the ecumenical documents have any official church status, either in Rome or in the respective Protestant denominations; and, as indicated above, the *ad hoc* nature of the ECT makes these documents in particular of no real ecclesiastical significance.[2] So what exactly has been achieved in terms of real institutional rapprochement based on officially acknowledged substantial theological agreement? Not much at all.

---

[2] The text of the Lutheran-Catholic agreement, along with related documents, is available online at www.elca.org/ecumenical/ecumenicaldialogue/romancatholic/jddj/index.html ECT documents, and some commentary, can be found at www.elca.org/ecumenical/ecumenicaldialogue/romancatholic/jddj/index.html the website of the thoughtful Catholic journal, *First Things*, edited by former Lutheran turned Catholic, Richard John Neuhaus, who, along with Charles Colson, did much to pioneer the discussions and the agreements.

Second, it is important to understand that the dispute at the Reformation over this issue of justification was not one of total disagreement at all points. Indeed, there was a certain amount of common ground shared by Catholics and Protestants even in this most contentious of areas: both agreed that justification was on account of Christ's righteousness; both gave a place to faith; and both saw justification as being by grace. The disagreements touched on whether Christ's righteousness was imputed or imparted; whether faith was the sole instrument of justification; and whether saving grace was, among other things, operative or co-operative, a quality of God or something dispensed by the sacraments. Now, the polemics of the sixteenth century inevitably tended to obscure the common ground, even in the most calm confessional formulations, as each side defined itself over against the other; when identities are at stake, dividing boundary markers are inevitably accented; but this common ground was really there on some issues, even in the sixteenth century; and thus any ecumenical discussion is likely to focus on this preexistent commonality and not on the real points of dispute in the Reformation. A question of emphasis, maybe, but when the common Christological basis of justification is accented, the serious and very real disagreements over justification that do exist between confessional communions can be quite effectively marginalized; and this has arguably been done, most notably in the ECT statement on the same. Sure, the words can be agreed upon by both sides: but this represents, on one level, simply an acknowledgment of preexisting common ground which was never disputed; at another level, there is a deployment of a common Pauline-Augustinian vocabulary which can be understood in a variety of different ways, some mutually exclusive. Agreements of such a verbal nature are reminiscent of the seventeenth-century debates about grace between Dominicans and Jesuits which were so brutally satirized by Blaise Pascal in *The Provincial Letters*. And it is an ecclesiastical-theological fact, not a pedantic historical detail, that Trent's teaching, anathemas and all, remains in force to this day; Catholicism has conceded nothing of that ground;

and confessional Protestantism, Lutheran and Reformed, found Trent unacceptable then and, indeed, regarded itself as clearly and decisively anathematized in its declarations. There is little room for maneuver here: either Trent was and is wrong, or confessional Protestantism was and is wrong, or they were and are both wrong. No other option presents itself; and each of these positions has obvious implications for everything from church affiliation to preaching.[3]

Third, the doctrine of justification does not stand in structural isolation from the rest of theology. On the contrary, it stands in positive connection to an understanding of the sacraments, ecclesiology, etc. etc. To bring out just one issue here: the Roman Catholic insistence on purgatory. Now, it is true that Protestants believe that those who die in the Lord still need to be actually perfected; but this is an eschatological point of little systematic significance. In Roman Catholicism, however, purgatory is not simply a point of eschatology but is closely connected to the Church's penitential system, the understanding of saints, and the treasury of merits. This is made clear in the Catholic Catechism which argues that prayers, penances, and, supremely, masses offered by the living on behalf of the dead help to purify those who are in purgatory and expedite their access to the beatific vision (Catechism, para. 1032), and which explicitly maintains the link between penance, purgatory, indulgences, and the treasury of merits (1474–1479, 1498).[4] If there is agreement between Protestants and Catholics on justification, if the

---

[3] The rather stark alternatives I have outlined here raise the obvious question of whether the Lutheran-Catholic agreement on justification is not simply being disingenuous when it declares the anathemas of the sixteenth century no longer apply. In fact, Avery Dulles has addressed just this issue in a typically honest and thoughtful response to the document and attempted to explain the Magisterium's rationale in signing on; yet his argument would seem to amount ultimately to the rather pragmatic position that, in a time when the church in the West stands on the verge of collapse, the enemy of my enemy necessarily becomes my friend: see his "Two Languages of Salvation: The Lutheran-Catholic Join Declaration," at www.firstthings.com/ftissues/ft9912/articles/dulles.html.

points in dispute at the Reformation were simply monumental misunderstandings or only relatively important compared to the points held in common, then why does purgatory, and all the doctrinal, penitential baggage it carries with it, still exist in Catholic theology? Its very persistence speaks a different understanding of the appropriation of Christ's righteousness, of the instrument, or instruments, of justification, and, one might add of justification itself—indeed, of the whole Christian life, before and after death—to that which Protestantism, even in its most attenuated forms, has typically held. And lest one dismiss this complaint as hyperdoctrinalism or as abstract criticism by an ivory-tower academic, spend a moment reflecting upon the different pastoral strategies which will be deployed, depending on whether or not one believes in purgatory, with all its penitential connections and implications. This should surely be taken into account when assessing how to act on claims such as that expressed by James Packer on page 180, that evangelicals and Catholics have "sufficient account of the gospel of salvation for shared evangelistic ministry." Purgatory surely remains one of the main elephants in the room when it comes to Catholic-Protestant agreements on justification.[5]

Fourth, it may well be true that most evangelicals no longer believe in the Protestant doctrine of justification; but that may

---

[4] The Catechism is available via the website of the United States Council of Catholic Bishops at www.usccb.org/index.shtml.

[5] In this context, I am also reminded of the argument laid out by post-Christian feminist theologian, Daphne Hampson, to the effect that Catholic-Protestant ecumenism fails to take account of the fundamentally different understandings of what it is to be human, with the former assuming a substantial definition of humanity, the latter a relational/ status understanding; and that any agreement to a form of words which does not deal with this basic underlying difference (which underpins the differences in understanding of what justification is—is it a process or a status?) is doomed to failure. Yet the ECT agreement on justification does not even approach such a level of theological/anthropological sophistication and signally fails to address such an issue. See Daphne Hampson, *Christian Contradictions: The Structures of Luther and Catholic Thought* (Cambridge: CUP, 2001).

not necessarily represent a point of strength or a valuable ecumenical opportunity; might it not rather be a sign of the problem of the theological identity of evangelicalism itself? Indeed, a very cynical and perhaps uncharitable Protestant response to this argument might be to conclude that Catholics and Evangelicals can therefore agree on justification simply because Catholics understand Catholicism while Evangelicals either do not understand Protestantism or do not care about it. That is certainly not the case with the authors of this book; but there is nonetheless an obvious problem here. Perhaps a more generous reading might suggest that this marginalizing of the historic Protestant understanding of justification is indicative of how evangelicalism as a coalition movement has moved from its historic Protestant roots to something less well-defined in terms of doctrine. And this again goes to the heart of the problem with which I started: the meaning of evangelicalism relative to its theological content is not a given; and that derives in part from the minimal doctrinal commitments or "mere Christianity" which its transdenominational nature requires.

This connects to another area in which the authors offer a positive assessment of Catholicism in comparison to evangelicalism: the Catholic Catechism. True enough, this is an impressive document which offers a pretty comprehensive account of the Catholic faith, and evangelicalism certainly has no equivalent. But evangelicalism has no equivalent for the simple reason that it is not an ecclesiastical institution but a broad-based, eclectic movement of various churches and individuals, bound together by "elective affinities," to use Geoffrey Wainwright's phrase, not all, nor even many, of which are doctrinal. As such, it is by definition incapable of producing a comprehensive theological document of a kind with the Catholic Catechism. To use a political analogy: the Communist Party could have a positive manifesto, because it was a party with a comprehensive political philosophy; popular-front socialism could have no equivalent document because it was a collection of disparate left-wingers bound together only by a shared dislike of capitalism, a doctrinally minimal point which could scarcely form the foundation for elaborating a comprehensive, positive political philosophy. Evangelicalism is a popular front movement, too, and subject to the same basic problem.

Of course, if one turns from the nebulous concept of evangelicalism to a more concrete, confessional form of Protestantism, then there is some significant creedal heritage upon which one can call for a relatively well-defined statement of what it is to be a Christian. Lutherans possess *The Book of Concord*, and the richness of the Reformed confessional heritage is evident from the collection of confessions and catechisms in E. F. K. Müller's *Die Bekenntnisschriften der reformierten Kirche* (Leipzig, 1903). The problem is that if one works from a broad non-confessional and non-ecclesiastical theological base which almost by definition requires no clear consensus position on important matters such as predestination, justification, sacraments, etc, then such documents are more of a source of embarrassment than of strength, in that they emphasize distinctives and precision, not a fuzzy openness and breadth. Indeed, at one point the authors pose the question in these terms:

> Is the Reformation over? Maybe a better question we evangelicals should ask ourselves is, Why we do not possess such a thorough, clear, and God-centered account of our faith as the *Catechism* offers to Roman Catholics? (p. 150)

The answer, I would suggest, is very simple and straightforward: one cannot abandon elaborate theology as a point of principle in order to build a transdenominational movement and then hope to produce something akin to the Catholic Catechism which, by definition, requires an elaborate theology to express; it simply cannot be done. And that takes us back to the problem at the heart of the discussion as set up in this book: we are comparing apples and oranges—a self-conscious church body, which feels no shame over its history and its clear doctrinal positions, and a transdenominational movement which cannot agree on more than the merest of Christianity.

This historical and intellectual coherence and depth in Catholicism is something which the authors highlight, along with liturgical aesthetics, as providing much of the context for evangelical conversions to Catholicism. Here, I find myself in sympathy with the problems described as part and parcel of some trajectories of evangelicalism (the reinvention of Christianity every Sunday, the consumer-oriented worship styles, the overall intellectual superficiality and banality of evangelical approaches to theology, to history, to tradition, and to culture); yet I still disagree with those individuals who see conversion to Rome as the answer. I would want to argue that conversion to confessional Protestantism is at least worth a glance as another option before deciding to throw one's whole lot in with Rome. Confessional Protestantism has a historic, creedal integrity; it takes history seriously; it refuses to assume that the latest pulp evangelical primer on postmodernism is an adequate basis for ditching the whole of its tradition; and it wants to take seriously what the church has said about the Bible over the centuries. As the work of scholars such as Richard Muller has indicated, confessional Reformed Orthodoxy, for example, has theological moorings in an intelligent interaction with, and appropriation of, the best theological and exegetical work of the patristic and medieval authors, as well as the correctives of the sixteenth and seventeenth centuries. Yet this careful scholarship is so often aced in the evangelical culture by popular potboilers which tell a very different story. Thus, post-conservative evangelicals may take the worst bits of Hodge, read them back into Turretin, mix in a faulty understanding of scholasticism as an adumbration of Enlightenment rationalism, repeat, Mantra-style, superficially learned and portentous phrases such as "Cartesian dualism" and "modernist mindset," and extrapolate from there to dismiss the whole of confessional Reformed Orthodoxy; but that is just one more example of the cod-theology which passes for scholarship in some evangelical quarters. In fact, as I repeatedly tell my students, if you hold to Reformed Orthodoxy, you can quite legitimately interact with and appropriate the best theology, West and East, from the Apostolic Fathers down to the present day, in your articulation of a truly catholic orthodoxy.

The tragedy of Protestantism, therefore, is not so much the historical and theological poverty of its confessional traditions, but the intellectual and scholarly poverty of much of what is spoken from evangelical pulpits, taught at evangelical seminaries, and published by evangelical presses (even those who claim the title "academic"), and which passes from there into pop-evangelical culture as the final word on the subject. Of course, in this context, no one has done more than Mark Noll to alert evangelicals to the seriousness of the situation. In book after book, by both precept and example, he has gently but firmly exposed the scandal of the evangelical mind and offered superlative examples of what real scholarship should look like. His own work is thus a testimony to the fact that work of the very highest scholarly caliber can be done within the context of evangelicalism, and the evangelical world is deeply in his debt; yet there are anti-historical impulses within evangelicalism itself which seem to militate against such truly impressive historical work really having a formative impact upon the way that theology is understood within evangelical ranks, and the way in which history and tradition can inform the life of the evangelical church.

To cut to the chase: what is evangelicalism? It is a title I myself identify with on occasion, especially when marking myself off from liberalism, another ill-defined, amorphous, transdenominational concept. But in a world where there are "evangelicals" who deny justification by faith as understood by the Protestant Reformers, who deny God's comprehensive knowledge of the future, who deny penal substitutionary atonement, who deny the Messianic self-consciousness of Christ, who have problems with the Nicene Creed, who deny the Chalcedonian definition of Christ's person, who cannot be trusted to make clear statements on homosexuality, and who advocate epistemologies and other philosophical viewpoints which are entirely unprecedented in the history of the orthodox Christian church, it is clear that the term "evangelical" and its cognates, without any qualifying adjective, such as "confessional" or "open" or "post-conservative," is in danger of becoming next to meaningless. And, even when one qualifies the noun in these ways, it is not immediately clear that one is then talking about subsets or modifications of a single, overarching, coherent movement. Indeed, there are many ways in which I, as a confessional, Reformed Christian, have far more in common with many Roman Catholic theologians than others who routinely claim the title of evangelical. After all, there are evangelicals who repudiate almost all the cardinal points of faith which Protestants and Catholics at the Reformation held in common and which were never disputed. Mark Noll is obviously not such, and his own vision of evangelicalism is clearly a gracious, thoughtful, orthodox, and, in many ways, attractive one; but I am not convinced that the definition of evangelicalism which underlies this book is strong enough to enable the realization of that vision or to allay my fears about the movement as a whole, if indeed it is meaningful to speak of it as a single movement.

The key to understanding evangelicalism in relation to Catholicism seems to me to lie in part in understanding the crucial difference between the Catholic Church as an institution with clearly defined doctrinal commitments, and evangelicalism as a broad, transinstitutional movement with a vested interest in framing its doctrinal commitments at the level of complexity which the coalition can sustain. The result is that evangelicalism as a movement will always tend towards an ideal of mere Christianity. And that is fine, providing it is understood that this will in turn always tend to attenuate evangelicalism's connection to the past and thus limit its capacity to draw coherently upon that past. In this context, one might add that the current predilection in some evangelical quarters for using the language of postmodernism for revisioning or reconceptualizing theology seems less a radical revolution in evangelical thinking and more the appropriation of the latest academic idiom for playing the well-established traditional evangelical game of non-dogmatic, lowest-common denominator, mere Christianity.

When I finished reading the book, I have to confess that I agreed with the authors, in that it does indeed seem that the Reformation is over for large tracts of evangelicalism; yet the authors themselves do not draw the obvious conclusion from their own arguments. Every year I tell my Reformation history class that Roman Catholicism is, at least in the West, the default position. Rome has a better claim to historical continuity and institutional unity than any Protestant denomination, let alone the strange hybrid that is evangelicalism; in the light of these facts, therefore, we need good, solid reasons for not being Catholic; not being a Catholic should, in others words, be a positive act of will and commitment, something we need to get out of bed determined to do each and every day. It would seem, however, that if Noll and Nystrom are correct, many who call themselves evangelical really lack any good reason for such an act of will; and the obvious conclusion, therefore, should be that they do the decent thing and rejoin the Roman Catholic Church. I cannot go down that path myself, primarily because of my view of justification by faith and because of my ecclesiology; but those who reject the former and lack the latter have no real basis upon which to perpetuate what is, in effect, an act of schism on their part. For such, the Reformation is over; for me, the fat lady has yet to sing; in fact, I am not sure at this time that she has even left her dressing room.

PART TWO

2.1

THE AGE OF APATHY

If there is a vice or characteristic that is often regarded as typical of the modern Western world, it is apathy, that lazy, couldn't-care-less indifference which marks out the couch-potato MTV world in which we live from previous generations. Whether it is low voter turn-out at election time, or the seeming impossibility of raising public consciousness on big issues such as world poverty, apathy it would seem rules the day. Apathy, however, does not exist in a vacuum but must surely be understood in the context of a number of other cultural traits.

First, there is materialistic comfort. In places and times where insufficient resources make life itself a battle for survival, there is little room for apathy. The peasant who has to work hard just to grow enough food for his family cannot be indifferent to the weather, to the condition of the soil, to the quality of seed he sows, to the amount of time he needs to work, to the price he has to pay to get grain or tools for tilling the land. The mother whose child is dying of malnutrition or disease cannot be apathetic about the supplies of food or medicine which she needs to keep the child alive. The worker who faces the possibility of unemployment and of impending poverty cannot take an easygoing approach to the standard of his own work, the financial health of his employer, or the technological developments which might change or even undermine his current role. Thankfully, most of us do not suffer from any of these uncertainties most of the time; and one of the unfortunate side effects is that we are frequently complacent and apathetic. At least, complacent and apathetic about things that matter; our material prosperity and security does free up time and money for us to be passionate about insignificant trivia—sporting fixtures, television programs and such like.

Second, there is a pervasive cynicism. The origins of contemporary cynicism are probably manifold. One component is, ironically, the free access we have to information compared to previous generations. The more we know about the world, the more we realize how difficult, if not impossible, it is for us as individuals or even as nations to make a great difference to the way the world is. Combine this with the frequent exposure of politicians as venal and self-serving, and you have a recipe for cynicism. No wonder fewer and fewer people turn out to vote at elections. What difference does it make? When the British Labour Party can spout policies so right wing that they would have made Mrs Thatcher blush, when all parties accept the basic unquestionable status quo of the free market and its structures, when it seems that it is banks and multi-national corporations rather than democratically accountable governments who actually determine the cost of living, why should anyone bother to vote any more? What difference will it make? If we cease to believe in the possibility of change, or our ability to influence such, we simply give up working towards these sorts of ends.

Third, the very form of mass media—whether television or the internet—militates against passionate engagement. The form is simply too egalitarian, too democratic, too incapable of presenting the kind of hierarchy of values which would lead away from apathy and towards activism about important matters. On news programs, political headlines are juxtaposed with images of war; horrific crimes stand side by side with stories of disease and famine from around the world; and the whole lot is rounded off with some "And finally" tale of trivia about a man whose dog can sing, whose granny is a professional wrestler, or whose neighbor has helped him turn his garden shed into a motor vehicle. The deadly serious stands cheek-by-jowl with the utterly banal, and both have the identical value of being newsworthy. This may not always involve a total trivialization of the serious, but it certainly introduces a strong gravitational pull, for want of a better phrase, in that direction.

Fourth, this trivialization and democratization of values and concerns has found its quintessential philosophical expression in the various relativizing ideologies which are frequently bracketed together under the term "postmodernism." Today, we are all, it seems, the heirs of Marx, Freud, and Nietzsche: claims of truth and of value are never quite what they seem but are always masks or codes beneath which other agendas—material, sexual, or political—are hidden. Few of us may have read Nietzsche and wrestled with his thought in any depth, but the idea that truth is merely an expression of taste or preference—a very Nietzschean insight—pervades our culture, from the halls of academia to the Oprah Winfrey Show. And if all truths and values are merely matters of taste, then there is little point about being too passionate about them in the public sphere—what's the point? Such would be at best misguided and patronizing, at worst an arrogant attempt to impose our will upon another.

This then leads to the key question for Christians: is apathy an option? Is apathetic Christianity a biblically sanctioned way of thinking about the world? Well, if my analysis of the major causes of the current popularity of apathy is correct, the answer must surely be in the negative. Apathy—whether doctrinal in terms of indifference to Christianity's truth claims, moral in terms of indifference to Christianity's ethical demands, or ecclesiastical in terms of Christianity's community demands— must be repudiated at all costs.

Think about it. Reflect upon the roots of apathy as outlined above. Should Christians be secure in terms of their material situation? Well, it is a good thing to have enough of what we need, and even better to have a surplus; but the Christian is to realize that all these things come from the hand of a sovereign Father. What do we have that we did not receive? And is it not true that the Lord who gives can also be the Lord who takes away—and still be worthy of our praise? It is not complacent self-security, but thankfulness which should characterize our relationship to material prosperity and to the God who provides such. Any other attitude undercuts in practical terms the reality of our dependence upon a sovereign God.

Second, should Christians be cynical? Well, here, I am inclined to offer a more nuanced answer. Yes, Christians should always be cynical of the kind of God-like claims and agendas of mere creatures. For example, no government initiative is ever going to solve the problem of world poverty because poverty is a particular result of the general fallenness of creation, a point which no technical or educational policy can ever address. This does not mean that poverty is not an evil which we should fight against; but it is to say that we need a realistic understanding of what can be achieved at a human level. So there is a sense in which cynicism is vital among Christians in order to avoid being taken in by the ambitious rhetoric of the world around us. But cynicism as a life philosophy has to be unacceptable for the Christian because Christianity holds at its very core the notion that change is possible, indeed, imperative—individuals must turn from rebellion against God and bondage to earthly idols and put their trust in the great I AM; and the fallen world in which we live must one day be renewed, evil must be banished forever, and God's creation must become a true and open testimony to his glory and majesty. Yes, the potential for change on earth is limited in terms of what human technique and capabilities can bring about; but Christians must acknowledge the sovereignty of the God who not only created out of nothing but who will also act again and again to save his people, and who will finally renew the heavens and the earth at the end of time.

Third, should Christians allow their minds to be shaped by the trivialization which the mass media and the entertainment industry brings to our world? Of course not. This can be difficult to avoid; we need to realize first and foremost that media are not simply channels through which information passes like water through a pipe, but rather they are constitutive of the information itself and how we understand it. We need, if you like, to be self-aware and to develop a critical eye for what television, the internet, and such like do to our understanding of the world. But we also need to be aware that God is not indifferent to earthly values. He hates greed; he opposes the proud; he seems, if you like, to set his face against everything which the modern West worships. And if we are indifferent to God's hierarchy of values, then it is not too much to say that we are actually in rebellion against God himself. To be indifferent to greed, to have no strong opinions about pride, represents a catastrophic failure on our part to reflect the mind of Christ. And if we do not reflect Christ's mind, then whose mind exactly are we reflecting?

Finally, relativism and philosophies of suspicion. Again, as a Christian I want to give a nuanced answer as to how far we should engage in these lines of thinking. There is certainly much in, say, the work of Nietzsche or Foucault to which Christians can say "Amen!" For example, the fact that, sometimes, convictions about truth are driven as much by taste as by well-reasoned argument, is surely undeniable. While there is a clear biblical case to be made against homosexuality, it is also true that many people just hate homosexuals and construct their arguments against homosexual practice in order to provide a rationale for their gut feelings. And it is surely true that Christians frequently use doctrines that are true in order to achieve immoral ends: for example, the obligation of children to obey their parents has, I am sure, been used by some parents as a means of abusing their power over their children. Further, all Christians with a solid grasp of human sinfulness know that even our best and purest actions are performed with mixed motives, and that, even in acts of self-sacrifice, there is no pure altruism.

Yet when relativism and suspicion become the most basic and universal aspects of our approach to life, we cease to be truly Christian. The Christian has to be committed to the fact that some things are true ("God exists") and some are false ("God does not exist"); that some things are right ("Loving your neighbor") and others are wrong ("Sacrificing your children to worship some god"). As soon as we acknowledge the dichotomies of true and false, of right and wrong, of, if you like, the absolute authority of God's revelation in Scripture and in Christ about who he is and what the world is like, then pure relativism is relativized and pure suspicion becomes suspect. Further, we can no longer be apathetic—what we believe about God and how we behave become matters not of indifference or personal taste, but of God's command and of divine imperative.

This is where I close: the tight connection between belief and practice. For the Christian, neither is a matter of indifference. I believe certain things are true and certain things are right. That places me under intellectual and moral obligation to think and to live in accordance with God's truth and God's morality. If I am apathetic, what I am really saying is that God's truth and God's morality are matters of indifference, they are of only relative or local importance, and that God is therefore not sovereign and I am not dependent upon him for everything. Like the church in Laodicea, I am neither hot nor cold, fit only for vomiting on to the pavement.

BREEDING FERRETS ON WATERSHIP DOWN

Teaching history is probably one of the more depressing activities in which one can engage in the current climate. At an academic level, the discipline has been in self-destruct mode for some time, losing itself in a morass of hyperspecialized narratives, nihilistic epistemologies, and general narcissistic "numptiness," to borrow an appropriate Scottish word. At a general cultural level, the crazy consumerism of advanced Western capitalism, with its craven idolatry of the new and the novel and its contemptuous dismissal of the old and the traditional, has made sure that the utilitarian disrespect for history has continued which was first established by the rise of the industrial and scientific ideologies of the nineteenth and twentieth centuries. All of this has served to make teaching history about as welcome a calling as that of ferret breeding on Watership Down.

The church, of course, should be able to rise above the cultural consensus; but such is sadly not the case. At the level of church practice, the abandonment of traditional hymns, services, and patterns of preaching speaks volumes about how the past is regarded by many as simply not connecting to the present, not being relevant to the needs of today. Now, as will become clear, I am far from suggesting that the way church was done in the past is to be arbitrarily absolutized as if ours is the first generation in history to have been shaped by its historical context. Yet I do want to raise the question as to whether the changes we see in church practice are all driven by a conscious desire to be faithful to the Bible or simply by the unconscious aping of wider cultural trends which we have internalized and naturalized to the point where they are assumed to be as natural as gravity. For example, in seminaries and schools of theological learning, church history now often occupies less space on the curriculum than other disciplines, while the massive growth of areas such as counseling—a subject which carries with it almost no biblical or historical warrant for being a separate part of ministerial training—is demonstrating in spades the church's inability to stand apart from wider cultural obsessions and trends. In terms of biblical scholarship, too, the often uncritical acceptance of the latest scholarly consensus—however, one might add, one chooses to construct that "consensus," itself a knotty critical problem—and the all-too-eager dismissal of any exegesis or theological formulation which happens to predate the current trendy watershed, be it Kant, Freud, the discovery of the Dead Sea Scrolls, or whatever, is eloquent testimony both to the power of the wider culture to shape reality and the childish fascination with anything that irritates the older generation. Today, there is nothing that more conforms to the mentality of the cultural establishment than the rebel without a cause. Again, the analogy with ferret breeding on Watership Down comes to mind.

But even outside of the self-consciously trendy ranks of the postmodern church pundits and the avant-garde of academia, traditional evangelicalism itself contains powerful anti-historical forces. Evangelicals, after all, are those who just have their Bible, who draw their inspiration not from tradition but from Scripture itself. In some circles, this is often simply the unreflective default position; for others, the perception that the Reformation was revolt against the authority of tradition is carte blanche for rejecting any reflection upon anything other than the bare text of Scripture. Ironically, the latter group often has a high view of historical movements and figures—indeed, the fact that it takes its cue from the Reformation indicates something of a historical bent; but this is often little more than hagiography. History is about spotting the good guys (and they generally are all guys, the occasional covenanter martyr notwithstanding) and the bad guys (perhaps a few more of these might be gals, Mary I, Mary of Guise, etc), and about assuming that the former simply acted out of pure fidelity to Scripture, the latter out of the basest conscious motives. In other words, there is no critical engagement with history, simply the extraction from history of pure biblical practices and ideas uncontaminated by the times in which they occurred or, one might ominously add, by the innate depravity of the agents themselves. Ferret breeding anyone?

Yet history remains important, especially for evangelicals. Whatever the popular evangelical mythology might claim, the Reformation was not a wholesale rejection of church tradition in favor of the Bible. It was rather a critical evaluation of church tradition in the light of Scripture which led to the rejection of some parts of that tradition, the modification of others, and the acceptance as scriptural of the rest. Anyone who has spent any time looking at the attitude of Luther, Calvin, and company on the creeds of the early church, and the traditional language for expressing theology, knows that the phrase "no creed but the Bible" can only be applied to these men in the qualified sense that Scripture is the sole ultimate authoritative epistemological source and criterion for theology, not that there is nothing of use to be found in the church's tradition of creedal statement, theological formulation, and doctrinal discussion.

The importance of history is, of course, central to Scripture itself, which is above all one extended history, where God, humanity, sin, and grace all have their meanings revealed in the drama of fall and redemption which unfolds between the Garden and the City. Yet, I would here beg the reader's indulgence by provoking reflection on the importance of history not by going to Scripture but by going to the thought of two men not usually considered by many Christians as having anything worthwhile to say to the church. The first is the German philosopher, historian, and economist, Karl Marx. Writing in *The Eighteenth Brumaire of Louis Bonaparte*, he declares:

> Men make their own history; but they do not make it just as they please; they do not make it under circumstances chosen by themselves, but under circumstances directly found, given and transmitted from the past. The tradition of all the dead generations weighs like a nightmare on the brain of the living.[1]

Men make history, but they do not make the history that they choose: Marx's point is that everyone lives at a particular time in a particular place; and that context imposes limits upon them, geographical, economic, conceptual, linguistic, etc. This is as true of the coalminer or factory owner in nineteenth-century England as it is of the evangelical at the start of the twenty-first century. To pretend, therefore, that we somehow stand outside of history, that we just have our Bibles and somehow manage to transcend our specific location in time and space when we read it, is thus hopelessly naïve, but until we acknowledge that this is the case, we can ironically do nothing to help us transcend our own time. A critical approach to ourselves and to the tradition in which we stand is only possible once we acknowledge Marx's point and accept that we are deeply indebted to the generations of all those who have gone before. This is bitter medicine for those who think history is all about good guys and bad guys, and who think that God's will can be read in a simple and straightforward manner off the surface of events and actions. Yet even a brief reflection on our theology tells us that this is a woefully naïve position. For example, until we realize that the word "Trinity" does not occur in the Bible and grapple with how and why it came to be used in the way we use it, then the first time we encounter someone, say a Jehovah's Witness doing the

---

[1] Robert C. Tucker (ed.), *The Marx-Engels Reader*, Second Edition (New York: Norton, 1978), 595.

rounds, who states the obvious—that we evangelicals say we believe in the sole sufficiency and authority of Scripture but then proceed to use extra-biblical terms—we are likely to find ourselves in something of a quandary. Further, unless we acknowledge the potential difference between our received tradition and the teaching of Scripture, we are incapable of critiquing that tradition. One more point: if we do not have a good grasp of the history of our theology, we will be ill-prepared to defend that tradition both from its enemies and from its well-meaning but ill-informed allies. All three potential problems can be mitigated somewhat by acknowledging how history has shaped our churches and thereby ourselves; and until we gain that knowledge of history, we are unlikely to see any improvement when faced with these issues.

If Marx's comment brings home to us how the uncritical identification of our chosen history with God's revealed will makes it necessary to grasp how we are shaped by the contexts into which we are placed by circumstances beyond our control, my second thinker highlights the importance of a knowledge of history as something which gives us a place to stand and resist those forces which would bend us to their will as if we had no choice. Milan Kundera, the Czech writer and Nobel Laureate, makes the following provocative comment:

[T]he struggle of man against power is the struggle of memory against forgetting.[2]

Kundera is writing against the background of post-Prague Spring Soviet oppression in his homeland when politicians who fell foul of Moscow were, literally and metaphorically, airbrushed from history and out of the memories of their people. His point is that the rewriting of history, even in extreme cases the deliberate falsification of history, to suit the agendas of the present does nothing other than disempower those whose history is being thus disemboweled. It is not just the Soviet bloc that does this, of course. One can think

---

[2] Milan Kundera, *The Book of Laughter and Forgetting*, trans. Michael Henry Heim (London: Penguin, 1981).

of the veritable industry of Holocaust denial that occupies the darker recesses of the Web, or the way in which the narrative of American frontier expansion has often been told without reference to the dispossession of Native Americans. Or, to bring the point closer to home, one might reflect upon the way the free market is often extolled in contemporary Western political narratives where its undoubted benefits are extolled but with no reference to the sweatshops, illegal immigration, and various acts of selective exploitation upon which the system depends. In each case, the work of historians who are willing to pay attention to the sources, question the unquestioned assumptions, and on occasion take the flack for speaking out, can bring immeasurable benefits to those prepared to listen.

This is a useful thing to bear in mind when approaching evangelical history. It is sad but true that there are those whose use of history is part of an agenda which allows them to manipulate the church in the present. This is particularly the case when it comes to doctrinal and moral issues. Claims, for example, that the penal substitutionary view of the atonement or justification by imputation or the inerrancy of Scripture are late innovations, and/or tied to outmoded social or philosophical paradigms, sound like very plausible and persuasive bases for "rethinking" or "revisioning" these ideas, terms which are usually euphemisms for "abandoning" or "dispatching to the theological dustbin." A careful study of the doctrinal history can at least demonstrate the erroneous nature of such claims. The same applies to those who claim that it is a legitimate, value-neutral move to build a Christology without reference to John's Gospel. When one takes seriously both the historical way in which the church developed the canon and then the historical context in which the Synoptic Gospels came to be separated from that of John through the development of critical history, the apparent innocence of the scholarly move is exposed as manipulative, philosophically loaded, and highly specious. Then, there are those who attempt to reintroduce old heresies as if they were new biblical insights: one thinks, for example, of those recent theologians who

114

deny or radically limit God's knowledge of the future. Even a cursory glance at seventeenth-century theological history will reveal that this has been done before by the Socinians; that their modern-day disciples seem so hesitant to make the obvious historical connection may have more than a little to do with the fact that Socinianism was beyond the Pale in the seventeenth century (and that in substantial part because of the Socinian view of God's foreknowledge). It may also be that a comparison of the incredibly sophisticated arguments of the seventeenth-century Socinians proves somewhat unflattering to their somewhat less rigorous descendants. Indeed, given all this, advertising your evangelical seminary as having representatives of Socinianism Lite on faculty is scarcely likely to boost your fundraising ventures. Far better it seems to airbrush history and present yesterday's tired old heresy as today's creative evangelicalism.

Such manipulation is scarcely the preserve of those who want out from under traditional theological doctrines and approaches, however: there is a great tendency among many who seem, on the surface, to have a great regard for the Christian past, to subtly (and sometimes not so subtly) write history in a way that can produce little more than self-serving partisan propaganda.[3] This can take many forms. There are those who can write thousands of words on a man like Martyn Lloyd Jones with scarcely a word of criticism. Yet one assumes the Doctor, for all of his great achievements, was still totally depraved like the rest of us; one assumes therefore that he did many things that were at least ambiguous in their impact and

---

[3] Of course, history is not identical with the past; it is a *representation*, in both senses of the word, of the past; it is selective; it constructs a narrative which may not have been obvious to the various historical agents being studied; it is thus in part at least a reflection of the historian him or herself. Yet I for one still believe that some historical narratives are more true than others, that, say, those who deny the genocidal use of the gas chambers at Auschwitz are wrong and are writing bad history in a way that a historian who takes the opposite stance is not. The latter person is without doubt having to be selective and limited in the way the history is written, but the narrative makes more sense of the evidence than does Holocaust denial.

effects; and one might reasonably expect anyone writing on him, even his staunchest allies, to reflect this basic theological fact.[4] Indeed, a study of him, warts and all, might well be more useful than a hagiography which leaves the reader either crushed ("I can never be like Lloyd Jones"), depressed ("If only the church had another Lloyd Jones everything would be alright..."), manipulative ("Well, the Doctor would have agreed with me..."), or positively dangerous ("Hey, maybe I should simply ignore the doctrine of the church as well!"). That the last few sentences almost certainly guarantee me splenetic hate mail merely proves my point. C. S. Lewis is another example: why is it that evangelicals have to make him into an evangelical in order to feel comfortable learning from him? He was not an evangelical, would have repudiated the designation, and is often useful to evangelical readers precisely because of his differences with the broad evangelical tradition. To have to make him—or any other great of the past—into something which conforms to that with which we are comfortable is both thoroughly patronizing towards Lewis and an act of narcissism which insulates us from allowing his thought to critique us.

It should go without saying that history, and the dramatic recollection of history, lies at the heart of the Bible. The whole point of the Passover was that it provided both a dramatic link with the past and an opportunity for parents to tell their children the story of the Lord's deliverance of his people from Egypt. In the New Testament, baptism and the Lord's Supper serve similar purposes, connecting the present with the narratives and actions of God in the past, present, and future. Yet evangelicals in our anti-historical mode seem prone to one of the two tendencies noted above: an idolatry of the new and the novel, with the concomitant disrespect for

---

[4] Strange to tell, Christian history is most often thought of by friend and foe alike as indulging either in hagiography or a tendentious providentialism. It is surely suggestive that total depravity is only used as a key for understanding the actions of those with whom we disagree, whereas it is surely even more relevant to apply it to the actions of our heroes if we are to avoid naïve hero-worship.

anything traditional; or a nostalgia for the past which is little more than an idolatry of the old and the traditional. Both are disempowering: the first leaves the church as a free-floating, anarchic entity which is doomed to reinvent Christianity anew every Sunday, and prone to being subverted and taken over by any charismatic (in the non-theological sense!) leader or group which cares to flex its muscle; the second leaves the church bound to the past *as its leaders care to write that past* and thus unable to engage critically with her own tradition. Humble and critical engagement with history is thus imperative for the Christian: humble, because God has worked through history, and we would be arrogant simply to ignore the past as irrelevant; critical, because history has been made by sinful, fallen, and thus deeply fallible human beings, and thus is no pure and straightforward revelation of God. It is this balance of humility and criticism that we must strike if we are truly to benefit from history.

As noted above, evangelicals have generally exhibited a deep suspicion of any talk of tradition as having any kind of authority within the church. This is self-evidently a reaction—and, on one level, a very good and proper reaction—to the kind of exaggerated claims made for tradition by the Roman Catholic Church. Yet we must remember that the Roman Catholic view of tradition is only one possible way in which it could be regarded as having authority or influence. Herman Bavinck, the Dutch theologian, notes a most useful distinction between the church as magisterial and the church as *ministerial*.[5] In the latter case, tradition is not presented by the church as the final absolute authority, but nonetheless the church here has a certain authority in helping believers to think clearly about Scripture, and in avoiding the absurdity of having to reinvent Christianity every Sunday. The church can err; its tradition can err; each individual stands or falls before his or her own master; but this does not render tradition of no account; it merely relativizes it somewhat. God has, after all,

---

[5] Herman Bavinck, *Reformed Dogmatics I: Prolegomena*, trans. John Vriend (Grand Rapids: Baker, 2003), 481.

made specific promises to the gathering of saints with regard to the guiding presence of his Holy Spirit which should mean that the church's teaching is given some considerable weight in theological discussions—certainly, as a general rule, more weight than the musings of any individual or self-appointed theologian. Given that the church is a spiritual, theological entity, listening to her creeds and confessions, and dialoguing with her greatest minds is not some optional extra, or a surreptitious retreat to pre-Reformation Catholicism; it should rather be a delight and a privilege, something which reminds us of our own relative insignificance in the grand sweep of church history.[6]

Being a historian may not be the most welcome profession today, given our disdain for the past, but when you see how the historically ignorant can wreak havoc with evangelical theology, the ruthless application of the study of history can be a welcome antidote to the lightweight, the idolatrous, and the heretical. Historians have tragically all too often been co-opted as propagandists for whatever cause is current in their day and age. Yet, ironically, in an age which lives in self-conscious repudiation of the past, no profession is more suited to offering prophetic critique than that of the historian. In the complacent world of the perpetual present, to look to the past, with neither naïve nostalgia nor cynical contempt, is to exhibit dangerously disruptive behavior. After all, to return to Watership Down: rabbits may be cute and cuddly; but they can also be diseased and flea-ridden; and let them breed too much and they destroy crops and damage the environment. Ferret breeding may not be a very popular profession, but it is sometimes necessary, even—or perhaps especially—on Watership Down where there are times when the only good rabbit is a dead rabbit.

---

[6] Given the promises made to the church in Scripture, it is clear that the role given to history and tradition by any Christian group will be intimately connected to its understanding of the church; that evangelicals have, on the whole, tended to downplay the doctrine of the church as part of playing up the significance of interdenominational parachurch organizations also helps to fuel an anti-traditional/historical ethos.

2.3

A GOOD CREED
SELDOM GOES UNPUNISHED

On the issue of creeds, the evangelical world often seems absolutely divided into two broad camps: there are those who are so passionately committed to a particularly narrow view of Scripture's sufficiency that they not only deny the need for creeds and confessions but regard them as actually wrong, an illegitimate attempt to supplement Scripture or to narrow the Christian faith in doctrinal or cultural ways beyond the limits set by Scripture itself. Then there are those whose view of creeds and confessions is so high that any other theological statement, and sometimes even the Bible itself, seems to be of secondary importance. Neither group, I believe, really does justice to the creeds.

I am very suspicious of both approaches. While I share the concern of the first group to safeguard the uniqueness of Scripture and to avoid imposing my own cultural preferences and tastes on someone else under the guise of gospel truth, I have a sneaking suspicion that the cry of "No creed but the Bible!" has often meant rather, "I have my creed, but I'm not going to tell you what it is so that you can't know what it is and thus cannot criticize it or me for holding it." Such is often the case with those evangelicals who reject creeds but have very definite views on the legitimacy of the consumption of alcohol and the nature of the end-times, for example. In practice, they effectively allow for no hypothetical distinction between what the Bible says and their own, or their church's, interpretation of the same. Thus, they render themselves immune to any criticism. Further, as soon as they use words such as "Trinity" or even consult a commentary, they reveal that what they *say* about their relationship *to* tradition and what they actually *do* in practice *with* tradition are in conflict.

I also share the underlying concerns of the second group for a high view of the church and of her public statements, and also for an honest acknowledgment of the indebtedness of Protestantism to tradition, albeit not in the same sense as Rome would understand. Yet the second group too is susceptible to criticism. In a strange way, their problem is similar to that of the first group: a radical identification of what the church says with what Scripture says in a way that makes criticism of church teaching in light of Scripture well-nigh impossible.

For what it is worth, I occupy something of a middle ground between the two groups (isn't it strange how most of us always think we represent a happy, biblical medium between two extremes??? Ho hum. Humor me just this once). I certainly regard Scripture as uniquely authoritative and divinely inspired; but I also appreciate the help which the insights of others over the centuries give me into Scripture's meaning and application; I also delight to identify myself with Christians through the ages who have worshiped the same God; and in this context I place a special premium on creeds and confessions for two very important reasons.

First, the church is more than just a collection of individuals; it is the community of those united to Christ and the community of the Word and sacraments, and as such has a special place in God's redemptive plan. Thus, I take much more seriously the consensus declarations of the church (problematic as that now is, given the diversity of denominations) than the individual statements of particular theologians.

Second, the *consensus* nature of creeds and confessions is particularly attractive and important. The fact that most creeds and confessions were formulated partly in response to political pressure is often seen as a bad thing, but I am not so sure that such is inevitably the case. Each year as I teach on the councils of Nicea, Constantinople, and Chalcedon, students express concern at the sleazy political chicanery that lies in the background of these events; yet the fact that a creed is formulated in such situations does not make its teaching of necessity less biblically coherent, any more than my total depravity inevitably undermines my occasional attempts to preach God's Word; and, on the positive side, it does mean that such creeds are no more exclusive than they have to be. Yes, they clearly rule out of bounds particular positions; but they are designed to keep as many on board as possible, and this ecumenicity of theological and ecclesiastical intention was arguably reinforced on many occasions by political expediency.

Given this, that creeds and confessions have, historically, almost always been documents aimed at consensus, two further points must be made. First, I am persuaded that such documents, particularly the early church creeds, should be understood in a broadly negative fashion. Scholars do disagree on this point, but it seems to me to make sense of, say, the Nicene Creed if we understand it as essentially setting up boundaries which exclude certain positions. In effect, it tells you what you *cannot* say about God without you consequently failing to make sense of Scripture's teaching. Thus, it leaves open a space for theological reflection, exploration, and even disagreement. The difference between this and understanding the creed as a positive statement of what you must believe is subtle but very significant. This way underscores consensus and inclusion; the latter focuses on precise agreement and exclusion. The same people may be included and excluded under both understandings, but I would still argue that the former is more appropriately modest and charitable and a lot less likely to lead to the usurpation of biblical authority.

The second point arising from the consensus nature of creeds and confessions is that they generally focus on the very core elements of the faith which command general agreement on both content and importance within the given constituency. Of course, they do vary in depth and complexity: the Nicene Creed covers less ground than the Westminster Confession or the Book of Concord, and I have argued on an earlier occasion in this very column for the fact that Christian theology requires a certain complexity of doctrinal elaboration and structure in order for any individual doctrine to enjoy long-term stability. But even if one takes the Westminster Confession as an example of an elaborate doctrinal statement, it is hard to imagine many Christians with any doctrinal bent querying the topics that are covered: God, Scripture, Christology, salvation, ethics, ecclesiology, sacraments, relation of church to society etc, Almost all Christians—Arminian and Calvinist, Protestant and Catholic, Western and Eastern—would agree that these subjects are important and that all churches need to identify their position with respect to them.

In short, I regard creeds as important because they are documents approved by the church, or at least by particular churches, and thus have more status than the writings of any individual Christian; they generally represent in intention a desire to reflect consensus among Christians; their negative, boundary-setting thrust means that they leave room for discussion, disagreement, and thoughtful theologizing, albeit within churchly limits; and they essentially focus on the real core doctrines. In sum, I might say that they give those of us who adhere to them a place to stand both doctrinally and historically, and thus to lay our views open for appropriate public scrutiny and challenge.

This leads me to my final observation: some of the second group I mentioned in my opening paragraphs, the high church party, hold so vigorously to the ecclesiastical nature of creeds that they find the whole idea of other statements of faith, of the kind that are now so common in our transdenominational age, to be at best irrelevant, at worst a phenomenon which undermines the importance of the church. This latter criticism is significant: ecclesiology is at such a premium today, we certainly do not want to add to the forces which undermine it. Indeed, it would be ironically self-defeating, for example, if the Cambridge Declaration of the Alliance of Confessing Evangelicals served not to strengthen confessional evangelicalism but rather to wound it and then to help in its demise.

I see the point of such arguments. Such statements are not ecclesiastically sanctioned documents, and by their very transdenominational nature they marginalize through silence or agreeing to differ many matters of vital ecclesiological significance—baptism and the Lord's Supper, for example. But it seems to me that two things need to be borne in mind.

First, there are precedents for this even within the strongly confessional tradition of Reformed Orthodoxy. The Helvetic Consensus Formula of 1675 was drawn up by the Reformed specifically to address issues raised by teachers at the Academy of Saumur, specifically a reconstruction of the divine decrees and atonement theory commonly known as Amyraldianism, after the French theologian, Moyse Amyraut, and also the denial of the antiquity of the Masoretic vowel points of the Hebrew Bible. It was not a church creed, but it served the purpose of allowing various churches and schools to identify themselves as protesting specific issues in their day and age. Thus, even the high ecclesiology of the Reformed faith is not averse to short-term tactical declarations of this kind.

Second, ecclesiastical creeds and confessions are built to last. As a result, they touch as little as possible on the local particulars of any given time or place. Of course, they bear the stamp of their age as do all documents; but the fact that Nicea still resonates over 1,600 years on, and Westminster over 350 years on, would seem good enough evidence that they are not so marked by the era in which they were produced as to have lost all of their relevance as the original framers passed into glory. But the church always lives in a particular time and place, and must always respond to the issues of the age. As a result, occasional documents, creed-like in form but much more modest and local in terms of their purpose, are extremely useful. On the one hand, such documents are ecclesiastical safety valves which prevent the need for constantly adding to the existing creeds and, almost by definition, making those creeds less catholic and more exclusive; on the other hand, they allow the church to speak directly on the issues of the day which are most pressing, be they matters of justification, public morality, or whatever. Yes, it is true that their often interdenominational nature could weaken ecclesiology; but that is only going to happen if churches make the category mistake of confusing such with proper creeds and confessions. The problem lies not in the statements themselves but in the fact that so many who use them have had no solid teaching on the nature of the church and thus cannot make the basic distinction necessary to avoid the problem.

Creeds and confessions will, I suspect, continue to suffer at the hands of friend and foe alike. The latter will always dismiss them as encroaching on Scripture's authority; the former will continue to make them narrower and functionally more important than they were ever intended. But on this issue I believe there is a middle way, which gives peculiar but subordinate status to such documents, and which also sees a place for occasional, transdenominational statements as well. The church must never compromise the unique authority of the Bible, must always focus on the basic essentials which cross time and space, but must also speak thoughtfully to the here and now. Historic creeds and contemporary declarations thus both have their part to play in making the church's voice a relevant voice. Until we realize that, I fear that a good creed will seldom go unpunished.

2.4

IS THE DEVIL
REALLY IN THE DETAILS?

Some months ago, Wheaton College was thrust into the limelight in circumstances which caused what can only be described as a nightmare for those in charge of the college's public image. An assistant professor in philosophy, Joshua Hochschild, converted to Roman Catholicism and the college authorities consequently refused to renew his contract on the grounds that his new religious allegiance was incompatible with the doctrinal commitment which every member of faculty is required to make in order to hold a full-time position at the institution.

The situation once again thrusts into the limelight not only the perennial issue of theological subscription at religious institutions, but also the problematic relationship which exists between Catholicism and evangelicalism in the current climate of practical, often grass-roots, ecumenism, an ecumenism which has been fostered by the prevailing moral ethos of the political and cultural tide at the present time. As the West goes to hell in a handbag, those who hold morally conservative or "traditional" positions on issues such as abortion and homosexuality have increasingly found themselves engaged in social activism which transcends—perhaps we might even say "transgresses" — time-honored religious boundaries; as a result, such boundaries have been slowly but surely eroded.

In an extremely helpful essay on the whole situation in the Catholic magazine *First Things* (www.firstthings.com), Alan Jacobs provides a thoughtful and thought-provoking analysis of the situation. As professor of English at Wheaton, and a personal friend of Hochschild, he gives a true insider's perspective on the unhappy tale which is particularly impressive for the way he offers a careful and not wholly unsympathetic critique of Duane Litfin, Wheaton's president, who was, of course, the man where the buck in this particular case had to stop.

What is interesting about Jacobs' argument is his treatment of Wheaton's doctrinal statement. As he points out, this statement must be not merely *supported* by Faculty (as would be the case in an umbrella institution — he cites Notre Dame University as an example) but actually *affirmed* by them; and the point where President Litfin saw Hochschild as falling foul of this was the need for him to affirm Scripture's absolute authority. Litfin argued that this affirmation should be understood against the backdrop of the Reformation and the evangelical movement, a reasonable point, given the authorial intention behind the original formulation; and Hochschild, as a good Catholic, regarded affirmation of the supreme authority of Scripture as entirely consistent with the official teaching of the Catholic Church. In this context, Jacobs also makes the obvious but important point that many Protestants, liberal Protestants, *cannot* affirm this and are thereby excluded from teaching at Wheaton.

In sum, what Jacobs argues with both charity and clarity is that Wheaton's doctrinal affirmations, taken at face value, are insufficient to exclude Catholics from serving on faculty. This is indeed the key point of his argument; the further arguments ,such as his claim that the Catholic tradition could well enrich Wheaton, while quite possibly true, seem more like appeals to academic or cultural emotions than the kind of argument to which a lawyer — or an institutional President concerned about his donor base — might listen.

In reflecting on Jacobs' article, it seems to me that he has put his finger on two important points: first, evangelicalism has traditionally operated with fairly minimal doctrinal bases; and the meaning and significance of such doctrinal bases is necessarily unstable precisely because they are so minimal. Hochschild and Litfin can both affirm the supreme authority of Scripture; yet the isolation of the statement from a wider doctrinal matrix renders it a formula which is, if not contentless, at least vague and ill-defined.

I was alerted to this phenomenon a year or so back when I was privileged to debate face to face the then-Wheaton professor, Mark Noll, on whether or not there was such a thing as a Christian approach to history. I will not bore the readers with all the ins and outs of our discussion, but one point for which Mark argued very vigorously was that the Chalcedonian understanding of Incarnation, as a point upon which all orthodox Christians agreed, could be a model for understanding how the divine and the human connect in history. I saw numerous problems with this idea, not least the fact that the Chalcedonian formula is made necessary by the very uniqueness of the Incarnation as an instance of divine-human action in history. Yet I also raised the point that no Christian ever "just believes" in the Incarnation. Yes, Catholics, Protestants, and Eastern Orthodox all hold to the Chalcedonian formula, but they never do so in isolation or in a vacuum. Each and every Christian not only believes in the Incarnation, they also believe that the Incarnation connects positively in specific ways to other doctrinal issues, from salvation to sacraments to church. In other words, the universal Christian belief in Incarnation only ever actually exists in particular doctrinal systems or matrices. Whether one infers the person of Christ from his work, or his work from his person, belief in the Incarnation as a metaphysical idea (that God assumed human nature into the one person) cannot be isolated in reality from related beliefs in a whole host of other theological themes and commitments. One can connect it incorrectly to other doctrines—hence the existence of a variety of systematic theologies; but one must make the connections, either implicitly or explicitly.

This is one of the problems with mere Christianity of the increasingly common evangelical variety. Evangelicalism, of course, contains in its very essence powerful impulses towards doctrinal minimalism. Some months ago I argued in this column that the transdenominational, parachurch nature of the movement virtually demanded such; to this parachurch issue, one could also add such things as the emphasis on the experience of the new birth as a primary locus of evangelical identity; the impact of the can-do pragmatism of the American way of life; the cult of evangelical celebrity, particularly powerful in the USA; and the eclecticism of modern consumerist culture. All serve to point away from a churchly, theological identity to something less doctrinally oriented. In saying this, I simply continue to beat yet further a drum familiar to many and point to the obvious fact that, in comparison with Catholicism or Orthodoxy, evangelicalism has a natural tendency to reduce its doctrinal base to a minimum. And that's why colleges such as Wheaton find themselves in a real bind when their doctrinal basis is shown to be inadequate to achieve the purpose for which it was originally intended.

What I have argued so far is that the isolation of a few, allegedly key, doctrines from their place in a more elaborate creedal matrix, serves not simply to simplify the doctrinal system as a whole; it also serves to more or less evacuate the individual doctrines themselves of stable and definite content. A simple, isolated statement about belief in scriptural authority is not enough on its own to distinguish Protestants from Catholics; a simple, isolated statement about belief in divine sovereignty alone is not enough on its own to distinguish Calvinists from Arminians; a simple, isolated statement about salvation by grace is not enough on its own to distinguish Augustinians from Pelagians. So far, so obvious.

Yet the problem can be taken a stage further. If such isolated statements themselves are evacuated of stable content, then it is arguable that they become not so much statements about God and about the way things are, so to speak; they end up as, in reality, little more than statements about human psychology.

Belief in divine sovereignty that is not susceptible to elaboration in terms of other issues (providence, predestination, grace, etc) becomes less a declaration about who God is in relation to his creation and more the objectification of that warm, fuzzy, and ultimately nebulous, feeling that somehow, in some way, God is in control and everything will be OK in the end—though one cannot then put any flesh on the bones by probing what "in control" might actually mean. And a declaration of belief in the supreme authority of Scripture becomes little more than a psychological commitment to the idea that Scripture is really rather more important than any other writing, though exactly how and why this should be the case cannot be stated with any clarity.

Psychology as doctrine is nothing new. It was Schleiermacher, the nineteenth-century German, who attempted to reconstruct Christianity in face of Kant's critiques and religion's cultured despisers; and he did so by developing in brilliant—one might even say structurally beautiful—fashion the idea that Christian doctrinal talk was really talk about human psychology. Schleiermacher is, of course, the great bogeyman of orthodox theology, especially in its evangelical variety. Yet the weakness in the trans-confessional evangelicalism which incidents such as that of Wheaton's removal of Hochschild highlight, would seem to imply that there might be considerable common ground in practice between the liberal theological tradition of Schleiermacher and the theological shibboleths of evangelicalism—certainly more common ground than either would care to admit.

The old saying has it that the devil is in the details. If this is so, then that's bad news for orthodox Christianity. Many church traditions have relatively detailed creeds and confessions; and the very existence of different denominations, so often derided as inherently divisive, frequently bear witness to the fact that doctrines, detailed doctrines, are important. This in itself should give pause for thought and, dare I say it?, even thanksgiving. As J. Gresham Machen once argued, it was a tragedy that Luther and Zwingli fell out over the Lord's Supper; but it would have been a greater tragedy had they been united because they regarded the doctrinal issue as a matter indifferent. Christianity is elaborate and particular for a reason: doctrine matters; and the Bible teaches a system of doctrine which can—indeed, which must—be elaborated. After all, it is only in theology's elaborated, particular manifestations that we can give even the individual doctrines any meaningful and stable content. Roman Catholicism grasped this a long time ago, as did those who wrote the Heidelberg Catechism, the Book of Concord, the Westminster Standards, The Thirty-Nine Articles, etc. They all knew that the more we subtract from the system of doctrine taught in Scripture, the less we are left with, not only in terms of the number of doctrines but even in terms of each doctrine's own intrinsic substance. This is one of the many lessons to be gleaned from the Hochschild incident at Wheaton. Both the Catholic professor and the president had a similar psychological attitude to Scripture; and the failure of Wheaton's founders to set the statement about Scripture in a sufficiently elaborate doctrinal matrix rendered it ultimately more adequate as a psychological description of attitude towards Scripture than as a doctrinal statement of what Scripture is and how it should function. To the extent that this is true, to that extent evangelicalism is vulnerable of becoming more of a psychological attitude than a true confession of belief in God; and that renders such a form of Christianity extremely unstable and vulnerable to attack. Indeed, when it comes to Christianity, the Devil is not in the details; on the contrary, I suspect he tends to live in the rather large gaps that mere Christianity's fear of detail tends to leave behind.

2.5

I Guess That's Why They Call It the Blues

I had intended to start my writing this year by waxing eloquent about Bruce Springsteen; but events have overtaken me, and meditations on "the Boss" will have to wait for a month or two. In fact, it was another icon of popular culture, Sir Elton John, or, to give him his full name, Sir Elton Hercules John (aka Reginald Dwight) who has rather occupied my thoughts these last few weeks. For surely, the images of him forging a civil union with David Furnish, his homosexual partner of some years, and then departing on honeymoon are microcosmic representations of the modern Western world, with its highly sexualized culture of celebrity.

I clearly remember some ten years ago being present at a church discussion of homosexuality where I made the case that it would never gain significant ground because the majority of people, many perhaps for reasons of sheer bigotry rather than careful thought, would simply continue to regard it as self-evidently wrong. Well, that was then, and this is now. It's not often that I look back on my life and criticize myself for being naïve; cynicism (a far less pardonable vice) is usually the error into which I habitually fall. But my attitude in the early nineties has, without doubt, proved to be hopelessly naïve. My only excuse is that I'm a historian and get paid to explain the past, not predict the future.

There is, of course, no single cause which explains why many of us so badly underestimated the depth of the impending problem or the speed at which attitudes would change. It is now clear, for example, that the hijacking of the language of victimhood was crucial. Yet such language only has real meaning within the context of serious, systemic persecution in terms either of economic or physical oppression. Now, while there are no doubt continuing examples of anti-gay violence, the systemic physical oppression of gays came to an end when homosexuality ceased to be a criminal offense. And it is risible to argue that the failure to extend marriage tax credits to gay couples represents serious oppression, any more than not extending such privileges to unmarried couples or siblings sharing a house together constitutes persecution of these categories. And for all the guff about negative stereotypes, I'm hard pressed to remember the last negative gay stereotype I saw on TV, at the movies, or even heard about in a country and western song.

Of course, in this context, the AIDS pandemic has no doubt played a significant role: on the one hand, the world is constantly being told it is not a gay disease (very true), while the disease is itself used to give real victim credibility to the gay community. Apparently, as long as you are a victim, you can have your cake and eat it. But such flip-flop logic is standard where homosexuality is concerned. Consider, for example, the existence of a "gay community" doing everything from singing in gay choirs to queer rock climbing to launching TV channels. In doing these various things, gay advocates constantly stress that sex is only one part of gay identity. The problem with this is embarrassingly obvious. On the one hand, those with same sex orientation do not wish their identity to be reduced to a crude sexual preference; at the same time, it's the only thing that unites them. After all, I love road and trail running and taking part in races; yet the sexual orientation of my running partners and fellow competitors is irrelevant to me, of no interest whatsoever, indeed none of my business, and certainly of no relevance to whether they run and compete well or not. The flip-flop logic of many gay people, who want to make their sexual preference simultaneously both the central determining part of their identity or community and only a peripheral part of that identity or community is unstable at best, utterly incoherent at worst.

In making my case ten years ago, I suspect I also under-estimated the power of the media to shape values. Now, I am far from holding to the reductionist, quasi-Marxist view of the media which sees it as all-powerful and the masses as hapless victims of its nefarious schemes. The relationship between media and public is like that between producer and consumer, one of negotiation, a carefully choreographed dance between what the producer wishes to push and the market wants and/ or will tolerate. Yet shows such as *Will and Grace, Queer Eye*, and the countless other programs which promote, sometimes quietly, sometimes overtly, a positive image of same-sex issues have surely been decisively influential in reshaping public opinion.

This points to the carelessness of much Christian thinking. Now, Christians have, on the whole, been pretty sharp at spotting the evils of pornography, simply considered. After all, porn is morally lethal in the way that having one's brains beaten out with a baseball bat is physically lethal: both the medium and its effects are crude, obvious, and actually relatively easy to avoid if you see the bat coming at your head and manage to duck in time. But sitcoms and prime-time network entertainment are deadly in a different way. As carbon monoxide creeps through a house and is undetectable until the effects are irreversible and necessarily lethal, so the drip-drip-drip of prime time slowly but surely dulls the moral brain cells of those who uncritically absorb its messages and its projected lifestyles with no awareness of how they are being transformed, even manipulated, by the propagandistic virtual reality to which they are exposed. *Will and Grace* and *Queer Eye* are the moral carbon monoxide of modern culture, killing us softly with their song, as Roberta Flack might say.

Yet there is one other factor which I did not anticipate ten years ago and which has proved remarkable: the desire of the gay community for social respectability. This has undoubtedly motivated the lobby groups and those who play identity politics as much as anything else. Now, I had always assumed that homosexuality, by its very nature, was a transgressive, risky venture whose main purpose was to break taboos and express sexual rebellion in a most dramatic form. To borrow Nietzschean taxonomy, I thought it was Dionysian in its very essence, a way of life rooted in a radical hedonism which broke through boundaries just because they were boundaries, and which knew no morality—at least, no *slave* morality— being beyond good and evil; certainly, this is the line taken by Camille Paglia, the art critic and bisexual scourge of the gay establishment; yet here we are a decade on with the comfy, middle-class gays of *Will and Grace* and *Queer Eye* providing prime-time entertainment on the network channels. While I confess to having never seen more than thirty seconds of the former, and none of the latter, the short trailers which flash by in commercial breaks seem to indicate that these programs show homosexuality in a manner about as socially rebellious as a Republican Youth Convention (and considerably less scary), and about as transgressive as an old folks summer day-trip to the Jersey Shore. And, to crown it all, now we have old Reggie Dwight, Knight of the Realm, no less, and his partner getting hitched to a media fanfare. Perhaps that is rebellion in some quarters, given the fact that marriage seems to have fallen out of favor with many heterosexuals; but it seems to me rather to be an attempt to be normal, to be accepted, to be *just like the heterosexuals*—or at least, just like they used to be. It is of a piece with all the puzzling hoo-hah in the Anglican Communion and ECUSA and the PCUSA where gays want to be priests and ministers of all things, the very purveyors of the slave morality Nietzsche so despised. What on earth is going on? To transgress social boundaries and yet to be accepted within social boundaries. To defy convention and to conform to those very conventions. To stick it to the establishment and to demand the privileges of that same establishment. How terribly white-collar and middle class the whole thing has become! Once again, the gay community wants to have its cake and eat it, it seems. Will the flip-flop logic never cease?

So how should the church respond to all this nonsense? First (and here I sound like a broken record), we need to have a properly critical attitude to what is going on. Of course, sinfulness of the human heart is what has created this mess; but universals are never that useful when it comes to interpreting particulars. Homosexual activity is sin, it is transgression; but then that makes the move towards gay marriage so strange. The drive to rebel and the need to be respectable here seem to go hand in hand, even though they surely push in different directions; and any church response needs to reflect long and hard on the Janus-faced nature of what is going on. In this context, I'm sure that we will find next to useless what I dub "The Simple Simpsons" of Christian cultural criticism (you know, the type who go into a panic every time Christians are sent upon *The Simpsons*, yet never ask how the program fits into the larger politics and agenda of the cultural system as a whole). Hedonism and untrammeled sexual license are clearly not sufficient on their own as explanations of the phenomenon. Dare I suggest that only a robust understanding of sin, and of humanity made in the image of God, can really offer a starting point for understanding the moral and cultural ambiguities involved in gay marriage?

Second, we need to see this as an extremely encouraging development. As gay marriage makes homosexuality respectable and safe, it will inevitably make Christianity scandalous and dangerous. And that is how it should be: the cross is frightening, disturbing, volatile. For too long it has functioned as a piece of costume jewelry, so it's about time it was once more an atavistic, disturbing force within society; and gay marriage is one sign that, in a sense, the world, fallen as it is, is returning to fallen normality. In the future, when the mega churches have finally become malls, when the emerging types have been conservative-and-liberal, Catholic-and-Protestant, dazed-and-confused for so long they don't know who they are anymore, when Reg and Dave are celebrating their silver wedding anniversary in traditional style, then perhaps those looking for rebellion, for an opportunity to "stick it to the man", will only have the cross and traditional Christianity to which they can turn. And that could perhaps prove to be the greatest evangelistic opportunity of them all. Till then, the situation looks set to get worse before it gets better; but, as Sir Elton once sang, I guess that's why they call it the blues.

2.6

BEYOND THE LIMITATIONS
OF CHICK LIT

A friend recently asked me to put down a few reflections on Roman Catholicism, whether I thought it was on the whole a good or a bad thing. The conversion of Francis Beckwith, when he was President of the Evangelical Theological Society (ETS), to Roman Catholicism has perhaps made the subject of more immediate relevance than might otherwise have been the case. So, for what they are worth, here are my thoughts. In this article, I offer a few areas where Protestants can learn from Catholics, or share common ground, and a few areas where the Protestants necessarily diverge from Catholicism.

I should preface the following by noting first that there is not much good confessional Protestant interaction available in print which deals with post-Vatican II Catholicism. Boettner's pre-VII work, a classic of its kind, is out of date; Berkouwer's account of VII is fascinating but flavored by the theology of his own later years; and, a few interesting collections of essays notwithstanding, there is no really scholarly critique of VII Catholicism from an evangelical perspective.

As a general piece of advice, however, it is worth avoiding "chick lit"—no, I am not saying that it is always a mistake to pass a Catholic friend a copy of *Bridget Jones' Diary* or something on the Ya-Ya Sisterhood; rather, I am thinking of the graphic novellas of the venerable Jack Chick, fixated as they are upon an evil and conspiratorial Rome, which are not to my mind the best resource for developing an understanding of contemporary Catholicism or for interacting with Catholic friends. The "cookie god," cartoons of ethnic stereotypes worthy of Julius Streicher, and disturbing images of attractive, pregnant ladies being tortured to death by medieval Inquisitors in quasi-Ku Klux Klan outfits do tell the reader quite a lot about the state of something, but not, I suspect, of contemporary Roman Catholicism. Contra Chick lit and popular Protestant shibboleths, there are numerous aspects of Catholicism that should resonate with thoughtful Protestants and which we neglect to our own impoverishment.

QUALITY CHRISTIAN WRITING

The first is, perhaps, one that is not always noted by those who think in strictly theological categories: Catholicism has produced the most stimulating literary figures of the Christian tradition, broadly considered. First, there is the incomparable G. K. Chesterton. Humor and irony in the service of theology? Can a Protestant do that? Well, Luther would have approved of the idea; its there at the very inception of the Protestant tradition; and it is a great shame we have lost it. If you want to know how much we have lost, then spend a few hours perusing the works of GKC who does for basic creedal Christianity what Terry Eagleton does for Marxist literary criticism.

Then for anyone wanting to wrestle with issues of evil and redemption, is there a better novel than *Brighton Rock* by Graham Greene? And to this one can add the names of Walker Percy, Flannery O'Connor, Evelyn Waugh, and (at least arguably—I know scholars divide on the issue) William Shakespeare. Tolkien too—though, as a loyal English Brummy, I myself tend to claim him geographically for the Midlands rather than theologically for the church. All of these writers offer literary expressions of various grand moral and theological themes with which Protestants should be able to resonate. Indeed, as a good Calvinist, I find myself more in agreement with Greene's take on human nature than I do with the sort of Pelagian tosh one finds on the bookshelves in most Christian bookshops.

A Shared Creedal Tradition of Trinitarianism

The second area is that of the creeds. Here, Catholics and confessional Protestants both share a high regard for the great ecumenical statements of the early church, particularly the Nicene-Constantinopolitan Creed, the Apostles' Creed, and the Athanasian Creed. Indeed, given the fact that the Christian God is not just any god in general but a very particular God—the one who is three in one, Father, Son and Holy Spirit—this common Trinitarian ground epitomized in the Nicene Creed is no small thing. Ironically, the explicit presence of this in the Catholic liturgy guarantees the obvious Trinitarian aspect of Christian worship; while much evangelical Protestantism repudiates use of creeds in worship out of a desire to be more scriptural, yet fails to offer any adequate alternative for safeguarding the Trinity in worship—and thus the explicitly Christian nature of the God being worshiped. As evangelical Protestants, we should humbly acknowledge our common Trinitarian heritage with the Catholic Church and make our criticisms of their liturgy on this point not by shouting the odds about the Scripture principle vis-à-vis use of man-made creeds in worship (most Protestants use hymn-books, not psalters after all!) but by showing them a better way, if indeed there is such.

Great Christian Theologians

The third area where Protestants should appreciate Catholicism is that of certain great theologians. Of course, it should go without saying that the early church fathers who provided the intellectual and theological background to the creeds should be part of any Protestant minister's or teacher's education, along with obvious later authors, such as Augustine, without whom neither traditional Catholicism or confessional Protestantism can possibly be understood.

But there are other, more definitely Catholic authors with whom every thoughtful, theological Protestant should be familiar. Thomas Aquinas is one, partly because he is without a doubt the single most important intellectual source for pre-Vatican II Catholicism; but also partly because his writings represent a classic statement and defense of some basic doctrines which Catholicism and Reformed Protestantism hold in common. For example, he is anti-Pelagian; and his basic statement of the doctrine of God forms the foundation for later Reformed Orthodox notions of the same, critically appropriated through a later exegetical and philosophical grid. In my own studies of John Owen, I soon discovered that to understand the mind of the great Puritan I first had to understand the mind of the Angelic Doctor.

Yet no Protestant reading list should end with Aquinas. The writings of Blaise Pascal are also a treasure trove: his *Provincial Letters* are perhaps the single greatest piece of satirical religious polemic ever produced, a devastating critique of both semi-Pelagianism and theological verbiage with which all Christian leaders should acquaint themselves. And as for his *Thoughts*, there is so much gold to be mined from his thought-provoking reflections on life and culture that these aphorisms are probably more relevant now than the day he penned them. Pascal sees through the superficiality of a culture obsessed with pleasure and with busyness in a manner devastating and astute than any other theologian with whom I am acquainted.

One could go on: from John Henry Newman to Etienne Gilson down to figures such as Brian Davies and Thomas Weinandy in our own day, the Catholic Church has produced a stream of outstanding theological writers who are worth reading; even at those points where the Protestant reader must part company with them, the stimulation to clarity of thought which they offer is worth its weight in gold. Indeed, I would argue there are few greater prose stylists in English literature seen as a whole than the great Cardinal Newman, a master wordsmith. And as for contemporary theology, I have for many years preferred to read the latest thoughtful

Catholic writers than their often all-too-superficial evangelical contemporaries. To listen to a Catholic like Eugene McCarraher on, say, postmodernism is far more stimulating, critically profound, and thought-provoking than any post-evangelical with whom I am acquainted.

Common Cause on Moral Issues

A fourth area where Protestants can stand profitably with Catholics is that of moral issues. Many of the current moral challenges which concern Protestants—abortion, gay marriage, poverty, social justice—are areas where there is a strong tradition of Catholic reflection and practice which can be studied with profit by Protestants. Abortion, right-to-life issues, and human sexuality are all areas where Catholicism and Protestantism share common ground; and the numerical strength, media savvy, and political power of the Catholic Church ensures these issues have a higher public profile than might otherwise be the case. It is worth injecting the caveat that, on some of these matters, the foundations of Catholic thought are not shared by Protestantism. For example, opposition to homosexual marriage is predicated at least in part on the fact that such marriage breaks the link between sexual intercourse and reproduction. Most Protestants (and Catholics!) already break this link through the use of contraception, and thus many Catholic thinkers would regard Protestant opposition to homosexuality as fatally compromised at the outset. Nevertheless, in the public square the practical policies desired by conservative Catholics and conservative Protestants are substantially the same.

Church Loyalty

A fifth area of positive note, and one where Protestants can really learn from Catholics, is church loyalty. For all of the concerns I have about Catholic notions of the church and of worship, there is one thing I find remarkable and impressive: the loyalty of many Catholics to the church and not to particular personalities. So often in Protestantism the attitude to the church as an insitution is weak or non-existent. Thus, a Protestant church calls a pastor whom some of the congregation do not like because they find his preaching boring or his family difficult or his way of running congregational meetings to be less than stellar; the reaction of many of those less than satisfied with their new minister is simply to resign their membership and move on to the next church—and to keep moving until they find a church which meets all their needs. What I find striking about Catholic friends is that the arrival of a priest with whom they are less than enamored rarely leads them to move on in this fashion. The local church is not treated as lightly as many Protestants treat theirs. Now, I am of course aware that some of the reasons for this difference in response are in theory theological; but in practice I suspect that Protestant wanderings are rather more to do with allowing taste to trump ecclesiology than with real issues of substantial principle. The ecclesiological loyalty of Catholics may be theologically misplaced; but the response to that is for Protestants to do better, not abandon ecclesiology wholesale as is so often the case.

These, then, are five areas where I believe Protestants can fruitfully learn from Catholicism. Now, I want to look at areas where principled disagreements exist. I hope I do this not with a censorious or pharisaic spirit, but out of a desire that there are points where Protestants and Catholics must part company because of sincerely held, cherished beliefs. Of course, these areas of disagreement are often historically and theologically complex, and cannot be dealt with in any truly adequate way here; so what I offer is, in effect, a short inventory of such which hopefully will act as a starting point for further investigation and reflection.

TRADITION AND AUTHORITY
Ask a thoughtful Protestant about where Protestantism and Catholicism most significantly diverge, and it is likely that they will mention the closely related areas of tradition and authority. Now, Protestants tend to be very suspicious of any talk of tradition as playing a role in theology as it would seem to stand somewhat in tension with the Reformation's view

of Scripture alone as the authoritative basis for theological reflection. In fact, the Reformation itself represented a struggle over two types of tradition, that which scholars call T1, tradition based upon Scripture as the sole source of revelation (the position of Protestants such as Luther and Calvin, and of some pre-Tridentine Catholics), and that which they term T2, tradition based upon two sources, namely, Scripture and an oral tradition mediated through the teaching magisterium of the Church. This latter was arguably the position codified at the Council of Trent, although it would seem that the boundary between T1 and T2 is in practice often blurred, and very difficult to define in any formal or precise sense; nevertheless, as a heuristic device the distinction is useful and it is really only as Protestants come to understand exactly what the Catholic view of tradition is (i.e. T1 plus T2) that they can come to properly understand how tradition (T1) does not subvert the notion of Scripture alone.

A moment's reflection on Protestant practice should demonstrate the truth of this. Every time a Protestant minister takes a commentary off his shelf to help with sermon preparation, or opens a volume of systematic theology, or attends a lecture on a theological topic, he practically acknowledges the importance of T1, whether he cares to admit it or not. A belief in Scripture as a unique and all-sufficient cognitive foundation for theology does, indeed, cannot, preclude the use of extra-biblical and thus *traditional* sources for help. Protestantism and Catholicism both value tradition; the difference lies in the source and authority of this tradition: Protestant tradition is justified by and is ultimately only binding insofar as it represents a synthesis of the teaching of the one normative source of revelation: holy Scripture.

Catholicism is more flexible. Though, as noted above, the boundary where T1 ends and T2 begins is not an easy one to formalize or define, Catholicism has proved far more open to the development of dogmas not immediately justifiable on the basis of Scripture, and has also been willing to take more seriously ancient practice as a significant guide. Thus, the practice of praying to saints has no apparent scriptural warrant, but was something evident very early on in the post-apostolic era, a point used by Catholics to argue for its validity (a good example of a T2 dogma).

The difference on tradition, of course, connects to other differences on authority. Undergirding Protestant notions of Scripture is a belief in the basic perspicuity of the Christian message. This lay at the heart of Luther's dispute with Erasmus. Erasmus saw Scripture as complicated and obscure and thus as requiring the teaching magisterium of the church to give definitive explanations of what it teaches; Luther saw the basic message as clear and accessible to all who had eyes to see and ears to hear. The basic Erasmus-Luther dispute epitomizes the Catholic-Protestant divide on this issue and also reminds us of why the papacy and the teaching magisterium of the church is so crucial in Catholicism. The problem of the Anglican, John Henry Newman, as he wrote his masterpiece on the development of doctrine, was not that doctrine developed, but how Protestantism could discern which developments were legitimate and which were not. By the time the work was published, Newman was a Catholic, having become convinced that the authority of Rome, not the scriptural perspicuity of Wittenberg, was the only means to resolve the problem.

One might add here, almost as an aside, that the canonical and hermeneutical chaos of modern Protestant biblical studies and systematic theology, along with the moral and epistemological and ecclesiological anarchy which it brings in its wake, is inherently unstable from an ecclesiastical perspective. It is surely not surprising that it has provided the context for some high-profile conversions to Rome over recent decades: Protestantism was born out of convictions regarding Scripture's basic perspicuity; the destruction of that doctrine can be read as an unwitting prolegomenon to a return to an authority structure which is functionally like that of Rome; and, given the choice of scholars or postmodern arrivistes or the Vicar of Rome calling the shots, it is not surprising that many have chosen the latter. The New Perspective on Paul is the most obvious attack on Luther's legacy in Protestantism;

but just as significant is so much of modern hermeneutics, representing as it does the posthumous triumph of the spirit of Erasmus over that of Luther.

OTHER RELIGIONS

One of the great mysteries for casual observers of Catholicism since the 1970s has been the apparent conflict between internal and external Vatican policies. On the one hand, liberal Catholic teachers, such as Kung and Schillebeeckx, have found themselves on the receiving end of very conservative internal reforms; on the other hand, both John Paul II and Benedict XVI have pursued what seem to be (from an evangelical Protestant perspective) a fairly liberal and concessive attitude to other religions, most notably Islam.

Vatican policy is, in fact, consistent with Vatican beliefs, despite the appearance. The Catholic Catechism is clear that the God of Christianity and the God of, say, Islam are the same God. This does not relativize Catholicism and Islam in terms of making them equally legitimate expressions of human worship; but it does reflect the standard Catholic acknowledgment of Christianity as a higher and purer form of the more general phenomenon of theism. Now, natural theology is a vexed issue in Protestantism, partly because of Karl Barth's belligerent "NO!" to Emil Brunner in the 1930s, and partly because of the persistent misreading of the Reformers and the Reformed Orthodox on these issues through the popular historiography of the issue at the hands of writers as diverse as Francis Schaeffer, Cornelius Van Til, and Stanley Grenz and their various disciples. Yet even the most historically sensitive reading of confessional Protestant traditions requires us to emphasize the centrality of the Trinity to divine identity and revelation, and to use this as a critical measure by which to judge other religions, such as Islam. For a confessional Protestant, if Allah is one, if Allah has no Son, then Allah is not Jehovah, for Jehovah is not god in general but God the Triune in particular; consequently, there should be no joint worship services with the local Imam, no blurring of the religious boundaries, whatever popular front platforms we might share on moral issues.

SACRAMENTS, JUSTIFICATION, AND ASSURANCE

The most obvious aesthetic difference between Catholicism and Protestantism is the role of sacraments, specifically that of the Mass or the Lord's Supper, in the respective traditions. Walk into Cologne Cathedral, and your eyes are immediately drawn to the far end of the aisle, where the altar stands; walk into St Giles' Cathedral, Edinburgh, and your eyes are drawn to the center, where the pulpit stands. The respective architects knew their theology, as each building focuses attention on the most important action which takes place there. While Catholics have always had preaching, they focus on the Mass; while Protestants have always had sacraments, they focus on the reading and preaching of the Word.

Underlying these differences of emphasis are basic differences of theology. Catholics see grace as coming through sacramental participation in the church; Protestants see grace as coming to them through the promise of the Word grasped by faith as it is read and preached. Then, allied to these differences are others: Catholicism sees justification as a process whereby the righteousness of Christ is imparted to the believer through this sacramental participation; Reformation Protestantism sees the righteousness of Christ as imputed to the believer by grace through faith in Christ. Catholicism understands human nature in terms of substance; Protestantism understands it in terms of relation. Salvation for Catholics thus involves a substantial change; for Protestantism, it involves a change in relation or status.

Much has been written, of course, about the basic agreement between Catholicism and Protestantism on justification, but the differences listed above are real and cannot be sidelined as minor aberrations. Post-Christian feminist, Daphne Hampson, has written of the failure of ecumenical discussions to address seriously the fundamental differences on human identity; and I find myself in basic agreement with her on this point. One could go further: the continuing centrality of the Mass, the persistence of Catholic catechetical belief in purgatory, and the Tridentine emphasis on human ability vis-à-vis grace, all show that there remain fundamental differences between Rome and Geneva on this issue. We share a common Pauline canon and vocabulary, and we share a history of Augustinian conceptualization of issues surrounding matters of grace and salvation, but we can only unite if one, or both, sides abandon cherished beliefs which lie at the heart of our respective theological and ecclesiastical identities.

Now, many Protestants cannot articulate a full-blown doctrine of justification by grace through faith, in much the same way as many Catholics do not really understand the Mass. Thankfully, we are not saved by commitment to a dogma but by believing in Jesus Christ. But the difference on justification leads to a fundamentally different view of the Christian life. For the Catholic, assurance of God's favor is a non-issue; indeed, assurance can be a dangerously subversive thing, encouraging moral laxity and poor churchmanship. For the Protestant, however, it is absolutely crucial: only as we are assured of God's favor can we understand his holiness without despairing, and do good works—live as Christians!— in a manner which is not servile but rather affiliative and familial. Catholics, and, indeed, Protestants who have a faulty understanding of justification are at the very least losing out on the sheer joy and delight of the assured Christian life.

I hope these few brief thoughts have highlighted some areas of agreement and disagreement between Catholicism and Protestantism. It is certainly not an exhaustive list: on the disagreement side, Mariology and Apostolic Succession are two areas I have not addressed which yet represent most serious points of disagreement. Yet, while I am a committed, passionate Protestant, I can still recognize in Catholicism much in which I take delight even as I see much from which I must differ. I have said it before and I will say it again: Protestants need good reasons not to be Catholic. Catholicism is the Western default position. If you do not regard the great confessions and catechisms of the sixteenth and seventeenth centuries as being biblical in their teaching on justification, then you should probably do the decent thing and become a Catholic. The implications your position has for Scripture's teaching, for church history, and for notions of authority, makes such a move a good one. Converting to Catholicism is not a crime, after all. Yet justification is not the only issue: if you buy into the theological anarchy of modern evangelical thought, then acknowledge it for what it is—a statement about the fundamental obscurity of Scripture's teaching—then do what Newman did in similar circumstances: turn to Rome.

If, however, you value the Protestant tradition on justification, and its concomitant pastoral point, that of the normativity of the individual's assurance, you may, indeed, you should, appreciate much of what Catholicism and Protestantism share in common, but you should remain at Geneva and not head to Rome. For me, the right to claim Question One of the Heidelberg Catechism as my own, as the most profound statement of a truly childlike faith and ethic, is too precious to cede either to the numpties of postmodern evangelicalism or the geniuses of Rome, even the great Newman:

Question: What is your only comfort in life and death?

Answer: That I with body and soul, both in life and death, am not my own, but belong unto my faithful saviour Jesus Christ who, with his precious blood, has fully satisfied for all my sins, and delivered me from all the power of the Devil; and so preserves me that without the will of my heavenly Father not a hair can fall from my head; yea, that all things must be subservient to my salvation, and, therefore, by his Holy Spirit, he also assures me of eternal life, and makes me sincerely willing, and ready, henceforth, to live unto him.

2.7

WHERE IS AUTHENTICITY
TO BE FOUND?

Some years ago I wrote a short editorial for the journal *Themelios* entitled "What do miserable Christians sing?"[1] It took me about thirty minutes to write, edit, and e-mail to head office; yet of all the things I have ever written, I have received more—and more positive—correspondence on that short piece than on anything else I have ever done. What was my basic thesis? That the typical Christian church offered the brokenhearted nothing whatsoever to sing in praise to God on a Sunday; and in so doing, the church was failing in her duty to care for the hurting, the downtrodden, the depressed. The answer I proposed was a recovery of psalm singing, not on the grounds that psalm singing is the only pure form of worship but because it offers a truly deep and authentic idiom for expressing the full range of human emotion and experience to God in the very act of praising him. No hymnbook or collection of choruses of which I am aware even comes close to offering what the Psalms offer in this regard; and for this reason alone I would personally be quite happy to sing nothing but the Psalms.

---

[1] This is reprinted in *The Wages of Spin* (Fearn: Mentor/Christian Focus, 2004), 157–63.

Now, one of the calls I hear most frequently from those sections of the church which have identified themselves broadly as "emerging" is for authenticity. Of course, calls for authenticity are a bit like calls for an end to poverty or child abuse or wife-beating. None but the criminally insane would disagree with such pikestaffishly desirable things, though it is true that there may be little consensus on how to achieve such ends. Nevertheless, whatever my reservations about emerging church theology, I am grateful for the sincere and well-intentioned reminder that Christianity needs always to seek to be authentic; and I am convinced that the Psalms should be a basic to such, not simply because of what they say but also because of the way they say it.

My assumption in all this is that human life as we know it is, considered in itself, ultimately a tragedy. Yes, many of us enjoy good times, have loving families, experience delight and joy, but even the wealthiest, happiest life ends in tragedy. Death is the boundary that shatters all humanity; it is a wicked and chaotic invasion of creation; and it condemns all of our lives to ultimate, unavoidable tragedy. I believe that this reality of evil and death gives life its tragic architecture, and that it should therefore inform all that we do. In my earlier editorial I argued that the Psalms should be central in public praise because they give divinely sanctioned expression of all human emotion which can then be used in the worship of God; in this article I want to expand on that theme a little and to argue that the tragic vision which the Psalms so beautifully express also demands that we broaden and enrich the ways in which orthodox theology is taught in the home, in church, in seminary.

The tragic truth of life in a fallen world can be expressed in a variety of ways. We are all probably familiar with the neat summaries of such which appear on bumper stickers, variations on a statement like "Life sucks; then you die." Not particularly profound, for all of the truth it may contain. It is, of course, essentially the same thought which underlies the following famous passage from Shakespeare's great play, *Macbeth*. In the play's fifth act, Macbeth, the man who has gained the crown of Scotland through murder and treachery, hears of the death of his wife, and he utters one of the great speeches in English drama:

Tomorrow, and tomorrow, and tomorrow,
Creeps in this petty pace from day to day,
To the last syllable of recorded time;
And all our yesterdays have lighted fools
The way to dusty death. Out, out, brief candle!
Life's but a walking shadow; a poor player,
That struts and frets his hour upon the stage,
And then is heard no more: it is a tale
Told by an idiot, full of sound and fury,
Signifying nothing.

The meaning of the two, the bumper sticker and the Shakespearean soliloquy, is basically the same: life is nasty, meaningless, and short. Yet there is a sense in which the latter enriches the reader's understanding in a way that the former does not. The language, the sounds of the words, the images, the alliteration, the metrical structure—all provide an elaborate and complex expression that draws the audience into a deeper, more frightening, more striking encounter with the absurdity of existence. Shakespeare not only provides us with a poetic manner of talking about an aspect of life which we knew already; in so doing, I would argue that he actually changes and deepens our knowledge of the same in subtle yet appreciable ways. Both the bumper sticker and Shakespeare tells us that life is short and apparently pointless; but only the latter actually confronts us with the full complexity of the truth and thereby transforms us in relation to it. The more we wrestle with the form of expression, the subtlety of the images, and the sheer beauty of the words, the deeper we are forced to probe into the nature of what is actually being claimed about existence in general and our own existence in particular. What is being taught is inseparable from how it is being expressed.

This is a point which I did not develop in my earlier call for more psalm singing in churches but which is, I think, critical to the importance of the Psalms in Christian life and experience, both individual and corporate. They not only teach us what to expect from life, and allow us to express our deepest emotions in praise to God; they also provide us with an idiom, a way of doing these things which allows us to understand ourselves better both in relation to God and to the world we experience around us. And, crucially, this is communicated as much through the poetic structure and language of the Psalms as it is through the realities beyond the text which the Psalmist has in view. As Macbeth's painful reflections on the futility of life cannot be separated from the way in which he expresses it, so the Psalms' teaching cannot be separated from the forms of words which they use; and as the images used by Shakespeare continue to haunt and to shape our thoughts long after the curtain falls at the end of the play, so the Psalms continue alternately to agitate, to provoke, and to soothe those souls which have soaked themselves in the Psalter's rich and poetic world.

This literary complexity is critical because of the complexity which evil and death cause for life. Death gives all human lives an unavoidable dimension of mysterious tragedy. To stand at the graveside of a child or of an octagenarian really makes no theological difference. Nobody should have to stand at a graveside for the simple reason that nobody should have to die. Mortality is an unnatural and unwanted trespasser in our lives, and it wreaks nothing but havoc both on the one taken and on the loved ones left behind. It is the most obvious manifestation of evil in the world, and as such the most problematic aspect of human existence. I would suggest, therefore, that it is impossible to grasp the full dimensions of the tragedy of evil, suffering, and death by simple statements of fact. To do so is to fall into the trap of reducing the truth about life and death to something approximating bumper-sticker wisdom: such slogans may be true, but they scarcely offer an adequate account of the subject in hand. This is where the Psalter comes into its own: it offers a full account not just of the range of human emotions but, specifically, of the range of human emotions within the humanly incomprehensible framework of a fallen world which cries out for salvation, knows that salvation is coming, but endures agonies and contradictions during the time of waiting for that salvation to arrive. The Psalms are brutally honest about the fact that, in this fallen world, against all that God purposed, evil yet has a reality which creates unimaginable conflict for human beings with creation, with each other, and, most mysteriously of all, even with their very selves. Human language strains to do justice to this reality; and this is where literary form and not just theological content become so critical. The poetry of the Psalms is thus vital to grasping the tragic realities of a world invaded by death and those countless lesser evils which point towards it. Bumper-sticker statements simply do not sound authentic in such circumstances. The confusion and tragedy of death and evil defy such literary reductions; authenticity in the face of these things requires the genius of literary expression we find in the Psalter.

The nature of the Psalter indicates that authentic Christian teaching, teaching which connects divine truths to real life, must therefore take into account not only the content, baldly conceived, of Christian theology, but also the forms in which this theology is expressed. The preacher can teach about evil, both cosmic and personal; but evil and suffering are inscrutable, and the complexity of the subject demands a literary form to reflect this. The poetry of the Psalter offers us a pattern of how this can be done as it draws us into its world, resonates with us, expresses and explains our deepest feelings and thoughts, and draw us into understanding ourselves and the world as it really is.

What is the practical implication of what I am trying to say here? I think it is threefold. First, and most obvious: the Psalms should have a central place in Christian worship, both privately and corporately. Martin Luther was once asked by his barber (or, as my kids would say, male hairdresser) how to improve his prayer life. Luther rushed home and wrote a wonderful little treatise on prayer (imagine that: the most significant and busy Reformer in Europe was yet so concerned for his people that he was eager to write a treatise for a barber struggling with prayer!). His primary advice in this work? Read the

Psalms privately, and if that does not help, go to church and listen to the Psalms being sung in public worship. The Psalms meet us where we are; and they take us from where we are to where we should be. That is authenticity for you.

Second, we should not settle for praise songs and prayers which are less honest and thus less authentic than the psalms. The Psalms give us a benchmark of authenticity which flies in the face of so much Christian piety throughout the ages. Too often Christians try to conform to what they *think* Christianity should look like rather than what it *is* like. For Dylan fans out there: which is more authentic, the sentimentalized material on *Slow Train Coming*, a product of Dylan's Christian phase, or the complex emotional bitterness of, say, "Like a Rolling Stone" or "Positively 4th Street"? Tragic that Dylan's Christian phase seems less authentic in its depiction of human experience than his earlier material.

Third, and perhaps most controversial, I want to suggest that the very existence of the Psalms require that those of us in the confessional, evangelical tradition think long and hard about the very way we teach theology. We are often criticized for our referential views of language and our propositional views of truth. I would fight to the end to maintain the important place which both of these must play in our theology. But as I hinted above, I think that the prepositional truth content of Christian theology can be dramatically enriched by taking seriously the literary form of the way the Bible teaches us. Again, I am not arguing for exchanging Bavinck and Berkhof for some fuzzy touchy-feely nonsense. But I wonder if, say, discussions of total depravity might not be dramatically enriched by engaging with the poetry of the Psalms; more than that, perhaps they might be enriched not simply by seeing how our great systematicians formulate the doctrine, but also how great writers wrestle with the issue in poetry and prose. Perhaps studying the character of Pinkie in Graham Greene's *Brighton Rock* or Iago in Shakespeare's *Othello* or Claggart in Melville's *Billy Budd* might offer Christian students of human nature some insights. Or what about the struggle between good and evil that all Christians feel within themselves? Again, we can and should teach this in a straightforward manner. But consider these verses from the poem, "The Welsh Marches" by A. E. Housman. Building on the image of medieval English and Welsh armies clashing on the border of the two lands, he moves to identifying these with the division he feels within himself:

In my heart it has not died,
The war that sleeps on Severn side;
They cease not fighting, east and west,
On the marches of my breast.

Here the truceless armies yet
Trample, rolled in blood and sweat;
They kill and kill and never die;
And I think that each is I.

This may not be the greatest example of English poetry, but the movement of the poem's image, and the rhyming of the couplets both serve to bring home the inner conflict with memorable emotional force. Again, the poetic richness of the Psalms, combined with the brutal honesty of the Psalmist's own self-expression, is crucial to enriching our knowledge of ourselves, the fallen world, and the God who acts to save within that world. Indeed, the savage anger about the prosperity of the wicked, the seething resentment of God that bursts forth in particular Psalms, the imprecations and cries of rage—all of these things strike a chord with all who have ever wrestled with the unfairness of life in all of its contradictions and absurdities. Such Psalms have a ring of authenticity because they are mirrors of the deepest, most tormented parts of our own souls. That the Lord legitimates such expression in songs of praise is surely an act of supreme grace and condescension; as is the fact that by the very poetic movement within these Psalms, he gently leads those who take these Psalms as their own to the realization of his gracious sovereignty. But there is more. Surely there is a lesson here about Christian pedagogy: the dramatic expression of these struggles in a poetic, literary form is significant and should profoundly influence how we teach theology in the classroom.

The Bible writers clearly appreciated the need for complex literary forms to give full expression to complex theological ideas and to the complexity of life in covenant with God in a fallen world. Theological curricula, at home, at seminary, and at church, should surely take the forms of the Bible's teaching with similar seriousness to that with which they take the basic content (to the extent that it is even possible to separate them). Only then can we avoid the reduction of biblical wisdom to bumper-sticker slogans; only then will our theology find authentic expression.

2.8

AMERICAN IDOLATRY

I start with a shameful confession. I belong to a family which regularly watches the frightful drivel called *American Idol*. All I can plead in mitigation is that my children are avid followers of the program; and both sons compensate for this failing by having otherwise impeccable music taste, involving generous helpings of The Who, the Stones, Aerosmith, Hendrix, and Zeppelin.

Yet *American Idol* does have a certain fascination even for a classic rock snob such as myself. As the concept was put together by one of my fellow countrymen, I cannot play my usual sneering cultural superiority card; all I can perhaps do is apologize on behalf of the British people for such a monumentally vacuous program, while perhaps taking some quiet satisfaction in the idea that it is some small national pay back for the US imposing *Friends* upon the world (apparently, this program is supposed to be a comedy; and if you believe that, give me a call—I can do you a great deal on the Brooklyn Bridge). Yet the show has proved remarkably successful: most reality TV shows go into steep decline after the third series; *Idol* has continued to increase its share of network audience well into its fifth season. Obviously, the mix of crass popular culture, the smorgasbord of variable karaoke, and the opportunity to witness the potential creation of a star have proved an irresistible combination.

Of course, *Idol* conforms to various canons of American popular entertainment, the most obvious being the lineup of judges. There is Paula Abdul, an attractive American lady who always aims to be as nice as possible about the performers. I suspect you could have Ozzy Osbourne (from my home town, by the way) with a sore throat singing *On Moonlight Bay* while gargling sulfuric acid and Ms Abdul would still regard it as "wonderfully sensitive and moving." Then there is a chap called Randy, whose jive-talking vocabulary is simply beyond my middle-class English comprehension but who seems (I think) to be generally positive about the contestants, though not to the same unconditional extent as Ms Abdul. Finally, the third judge is someone called Simon. He's English. Need I say more? The nationality gives it away: he's the hard man, the one who calls it as he sees it, the one who reduces contestants to tears. In other words, in the American context, he's the bad guy.

This is, of course, standard fare in American popular culture. The ethnic group which American popular culture most consistently portrays in terms of negative stereotypes is undoubtedly the English. From George Sanders as Shere Khan in *The Jungle Book* to Jeremy Irons as Scar in *The Lion King* to the latest villain in 24 (who's meant to be Russian, but still has a cutglass Anglo accent. What a surprise!) to Sean Bean and Clive Lloyd in just about anything, the English guy is always the evil one. Not evil in the chainsaw-wielding psycho way; rather, evil in the "I have an inscrutably devious and malicious plan to take over the whole world" sense of the word. It rather spoils whodunits over here—as soon as you hear the English accent, you know exactly whodunit, even if "it" hasn't been "dun" yet. If ever the ACLU were to file a class action, English exiles in the US such as myself would rake in a small fortune for the emotional damage and social disadvantage that such persistent media prejudice has produced. Until that day of justice, however, my own philosophy is that of the Roman emperor, Caligula: let them hate us, so long as they fear us.

This Simon character is significant in other ways, however, beyond that of the token English hate figure. For a start, he's about as interested in engaging in "aesthetic conversation" as Moses, Jeremiah, or the Apostle Paul were in "theological conversation." Love him or hate him, he knows what middle America will buy when it comes to easy listening pap and what it will leave on the shelf. The majority of sub-Shatnerian cover versions which form the staple of *Idol* get the rough edge of his tongue; the occasionally technically good but bland performance can expect the merest of passes. Americans may wince at the bluntness of his assessments, but their subsequent voting patterns indicate that they generally agree with his analyses.

I suspect there are two aspects of *Idol* which have served to make it such a success. The first is that it points very clearly to the cult of fame and celebrity that so fascinates the modern West. In the televised interviews with the contestants a couple of points emerge as particularly striking. First, the contestants want to be famous; and, second, almost all of them feel they are especially destined to be so. This second point, I think, accounts for the fact that they rarely offer any profound rationale for the first. None of them ever seems to ask why they want to be famous, why fame is such a desirable thing. Money might be the obvious answer; but, of course, one can make money, lots of money, without being famous, and in so doing have none of the problems which fame brings in its wake. So money can, I think, be discounted as the primary motivation, however much of a collateral bonus it might be. Instead, I would argue that their ambition is the result of them having been raised in a culture where fame and celebrity are unquestioned values, self-evidently desirable in and of themselves. Then, the contestants have also grown up in a world where personal value, purpose, and self-worth are increasingly understood in solipsistic terms. The whole rationale of libertarian consumerism, upon which our Western economies basically depend, focuses on the centrality of the individual, and his or her needs, as the primary locus of value and meaning. The end result of this is narcissism, the notion that I am singularly important in the grand scheme of things; and consequently anyone who attempts to relativize me, my abilities, or my needs is blaspheming the god-like importance my narcissism leads me to ascribe to myself. In the context of *Idol*, this narcissism comes to public fruition. *American Idol* is, in other words, a wonderful context for observing American idolatry, the idolatry of the self.

This is most acutely obvious, of course, in the hilariously self-important no-hopers in the early auditions whose singing is as tuneless as it is loud, and yet who earnestly believe that they are the next Elvis Presley, primarily, it seems, because their tone-deaf mothers told them so. The self-delusion is often positively scary; but it is entirely consistent with the narcissistic world we have created, where criticism is always deemed oppressive, nobody ever seems to grow up, and the difference between good and bad becomes merely a matter of personal preference. To say otherwise, to "do a Simon," so to speak, to call rubbish by its proper name, is to opt out of the conversation, to exhibit dogmatic arrogance, to make oneself a reactionary curmudgeon. Yet idols, being dumb creations of the human mind, are never very good conversation partners; and one cannot therefore solve the problem by having a chat with them; one can only solve the problem by smashing them, whether with sticks, stones, or, deadliest of all, words.

Yet if what I have said so far explains the attraction of *Idol* to the contestants and their families, what of the second point which explains its attractiveness? How is one to account for its spectacular viewing figures? The viewer, after all, gains nothing from watching. Of course, some are probably attracted by the vicarious thrills of seeing others fulfill their dreams, but I have a darker explanation: I think it is the pleasure of watching others fail, of having their dreams torn down, of being crushed by the cutting comments of the English hard man on the panel that exerts the attraction. It was George Orwell who said that all human beings are either masochists or sadists; and I have a sneaking suspicion that most of us incline strongly to the latter rather than the former. It is the weekly spectacle of seeing more wannabes biting the dust which keeps everyone tuning in, episode after episode. Indeed, I confess it: I like nothing more than seeing the fresh-faced Jessica or Mary-Lou or Brad or Chad having their hopes of stardom ripped from their hands and then being dispatched back to supermarket checkouts from whence they came. Nasty, but true. To quote two sayings of the cynic's cynic, Gore Vidal: it is not enough to succeed; others must fail; and (perhaps even more horribly honest) every time I hear of the success of a friend, a little piece of me dies. *Idol* plays unashamedly to such basic instincts, instincts found in all of us.

Seen in this light, *Idol*, both for contestants and for viewers, is a kind of trivial microcosm of the world as we now live in it, a world where the harmony between Creator and creation, and between one creature and another, has been severely disrupted. That's why it is so successful, and why reflection upon it is so instructive. Torn between wanting to be gods ourselves, and desiring to see all other pretenders to the throne cast down from their pedestals, we see in *Idol* the way the world is as we would wish it to be, played out in the comfort of our living rooms for our own entertainment. If you want to understand the modern West, watch the program and observe the overweening narcissism of the contestants (particularly in the early rounds!); and if you want to understand what makes you tick, reflect upon what exactly it is in the program which is so attractive. Is it Buzz from Omaha dismembering Aerosmith's *Dream On*? Is it Dionna from Detroit trying her best at *R-E-S-P-E-C-T*? Or is it something deeper, darker, much more pleasurable but far more sinister within your own heart?

The idolatry embodied in *American Idol* is thus twofold. First, that of the contestants, who want fame as if fame was something worth the effort. Yet fame is only so to the extent that it deceives us into thinking we are indispensable and important, as it allows us to realize our latent idolatry of self. Second, that of the viewer, who rejoices at the sight of others being told, in no uncertain terms, that they are talentless, dispensable laughingstocks, that they are not, in short, gods. Not as good as being god yourself, of course, but seeing others denied divinity is probably the next best thing.

I have said it many times in class, and now I write it in my column: the key to understanding and critiquing so much of human culture is total depravity. The drive to be like God is that which brought Adam to grief in the Garden of Eden; the desperation engendered by the success of a sibling was what drove Cain to murder. We might be more polite and superficially respectable than these two, but so many aspects of our culture, even trivia like *American Idol*, indicate that the central concerns of fallen human nature remain stubbornly intact, even in our most apparently harmless pursuits.

So what can we learn from this? Two things: behold the darkness of the unredeemed human heart, even in the small things. And, if you really want to make money in America, invent a TV program which capitalizes on idolatry. Oh, and if you decide on the latter and want some nasty English type to play the hate figure, just give me a call.

2.9

THOUGHTS ON THE RETURN TO ROME
OF PROFESSOR BECKWITH

The stunning news of another high-profile conversion to Rome is made even more surprising by the particular identity of the convert: Francis J. Beckwith, the President of the Evangelical Theological Society. Beckwith, who was brought up as a Catholic and became an evangelical, has returned to the Church of his youth.[1] What started as something which could have been simply a mischievous blog rumor has indeed proved to be true. Blogs telling the truth? Perhaps I need to nuance my opinion of blogging after all. Maybe some people have been believing mine all along. Scary thought, that one.

Let me begin by saying that I have tremendous respect for Professor Beckwith's integrity in making this move. Given his position, and, presumably, the fact that this move could well jeopardize his career, not to mention many friendships, he has made a difficult but honorable decision. It would probably have been much easier for him just to hide his intellectual and

---

[1] At the time of writing, Professor Beckwith's explanation for his move can be found at www.elca.org/ecumenical/ecumenicaldialogue/romancatholic/jddj/index.html

spiritual change. That the timing was precipitated (and thus made more difficult for him) by the request of a nephew who had wandered from the church and returned and wanted him to act as sponsor at his first Mass is a touching detail which only increases respect for Beckwith's humanity.

As to the details of his change, I think the key paragraph in his testimony is not one that deals with the ETS dilemma, but one which outlines the last months of his spiritual pilgrimage:

> The past four months have moved quickly for me and my wife. As you probably know, my work in philosophy, ethics, and theology has always been Catholic friendly, but I would have never predicted that I would return to the Church, for there seemed to me too many theological and ecclesiastical issues that appeared insurmountable. However, in January, at the suggestion of a dear friend, I began reading the Early Church Fathers as well as some of the more sophisticated works on justification by Catholic authors. I became convinced that the Early Church is more Catholic than Protestant and that the Catholic view of justification, correctly understood, is biblically and historically defensible. Even though I also believe that the Reformed view is biblically and historically defensible, I think the Catholic view has more explanatory power to account for both all the biblical texts on justification as well as the church's historical understanding of salvation prior to the Reformation all the way back to the ancient church of the first few centuries. Moreover, much of what I have taken for granted as a Protestant—e.g. the catholic creeds, the doctrines of the Trinity and the Incarnation, the Christian understanding of man, and the canon of Scripture—is the result of a Church that made judgments about these matters and on which non-Catholics, including Evangelicals, have declared and grounded their Christian orthodoxy in a world hostile to it. Given these considerations, I thought it wise for me to err on the side of the Church with historical and theological continuity with the first generations of Christians that followed Christ's Apostles.

Several points stand out. First, the role of patristic writings. Second, the issue of justification. Third, the common theological ground of Catholicism and Protestantism as having been originally determined by the church. Fourth, the weight of all this evidence pointing to the "safer bet" option of backing the Catholic Church. I can only throw out a few brief thoughts on each but here they are, for what they are worth.

As to patristic writings being more Catholic than Protestant, I would be the first to concede that modern evangelicalism has not been strong in its study and use of patristic authors, unlike the great founders of Protestantism such as Oecolampadius, Calvin, Owen, etc. This is a great and serious fault and places evangelicalism in serious danger of not being Catholic in the best and true sense. But to argue that the patristic authors are more Catholic than Protestant is arguably to impose anachronistic categories upon the first five centuries. Further, given the variegated nature even of the extant patristic writings, it is to beg questions of the kind: which authors? Whose theology? The temptation for both Catholics and Protestants has always been to prioritize those writers most conformable with their own later traditions. In general, many of the earliest patristic statements, for example about church government, are ambiguous and could be read as consistent with a variety of later ecclesiologies. I know those who read the Apostolic Fathers as pointing clearly towards later episcopacy; but to me they make statements entirely compatible with presbyterian polity. Truth be told: we lack the context to make a definite judgment one way or the other. Then there are the typical knotty problems relative to how one defines Catholicism in order to find it in the early writings. For example, the relative late date of clear Roman supremacy (scarcely a peripheral Catholic dogma) makes the earliest patristic writings arguably very un-Catholic in the Roman sense. And what of Mariology? The link between the penitential system and purgatory? The intercession of saints? All might be hinted at in some early church documents but one can only trace such lines once the later Catholic Church is presupposed. This was precisely the dilemma faced by John Henry Newman as he researched and wrote his magisterial masterpiece on the development of doctrine, and the reason why he was a Catholic by the time he published it. In other words, the real issue of how to read the early church fathers is, for Beckwith as for Newman, a matter of church authority.

This is surely again the case with justification. The problem with tackling pre-Reformation views of justification is, of course, that the church strictly speaking had no view: the Reformation crisis itself precipitates the first elaborate formulation of justification by the Catholic Church at the Council of Trent, a decree which then imposed order on the Catholic Church's dogmas in this area. The question of precedents for, say, Luther's position, is a vexed one and Beckwith is right to ask where this was before the Reformation. But that is, of course, only a potentially insurmountable problem from the perspective of Tridentine Catholicism. Catholic doctrine develops, as Newman made clear, and could have developed into Luther (as the work of, say, Heiko Oberman on late medieval nominalism has shown). That it did not do so points us again not so much to specific problems in the history of dogma per se, but to the issue of church authority.

I also confess at this point to being perplexed that Professor Beckwith regards both Catholic and Reformed notions of justification as historically and biblically defensible, the balance being tipped, it seems, by the fact that the former is more so. There are many questions one could raise here but two will suffice. First, Catholic and Protestant views of justification do share a vast amount in common, particularly in terms of a common christological basis in the righteousness of Christ. Indeed, such was never an issue in the Reformation. But the key differences—impartation versus imputation, and the instrumentality of faith—are mutually exclusive. One has got to be wrong, both may be wrong, but both cannot be right. Again, the issue seems ultimately to be one of the nature of church authority in making the final decision about something unclear in Scripture. I could go on at this point to my second point: the whole issue of assurance—surely the pastoral issue vis-à-vis justification at the Reformation—is critical. There is no assurance as Protestants understand it in the Roman Church; and Catholics regard Protestant teaching on assurance as leading directly to antinomianism and presumption. This is not a little matter; it is decisive for everything from the role of the church to the shape of individual piety. But, if Beckwith genuinely sees Scripture as ambiguous or unclear on this, he is right to return to Rome: first, justification is historically nonnegotiable to Protestantism; and, second, he clearly sees the need either for church authority or some extra-biblical revelation to break the tie—both of which really require a Roman understanding of Scripture and authority. His move back to Rome on this issue alone would thus be a necessary one of great personal integrity even if no other issues were causing him difficulty.

As to the third point, I do indeed rejoice in the common creedal heritage of Catholicism and Protestantism. But I do not believe the creeds because the church approved them. Now, let me nuance that. I find myself in basic agreement with Heiko Oberman on the nature of the Reformation struggle over authority. He argued that the clash between Rome and Protestants was not a clash between tradition and Scripture alone, but a struggle over the nature of tradition. Protestants (and, indeed, some Catholics at that point) held to the notion that there was one source of revelation from which the church's tradition flowed, namely, Scripture; and that this tradition (which Oberman calls T1) was thus always in priniciple corrigible by Scripture. There were others in the Catholic Church, however, who argued for a two-source theory of tradition, scripture and extra-scriptural revelation as recognized or defined by the church (T2), a position codified at Trent. This distinction is important as it allows me, as a Protestant, to acknowledge my debt to tradition in an honest and realistic manner without me being required to submit to the church as ultimate authority. My approach to creeds, therefore, is decidedly that of a T1 adherent: I take them very seriously because they are the work of the church at a corporate level, but, ultimately, I believe them only because they seem to have done the job of providing categories, concepts, and language which have made sense of Scripture for at least 1,500 years and continue so to do. Thus, they command my adherence but no longer and no further than they continue to be a credible and consistent synthesis of what Scripture says.

This brings us to Professor Beckwith's last point: the Erasmian move. In 1525, Luther clashes with Erasmus over the nature of the agency of the human will in salvation. The debate is often read simply as a rerun of Augustine versus Pelagius, but it is, in fact, far more subtle than that. What Erasmus is arguing is that Scripture's teaching is unclear and uncertain; therefore, we should keep speculation to a minimum and stick with the church. For Luther, on the contrary, Scripture is clear on such central matters as the will (and the nature of God, the Incarnation, etc) and we should therefore proclaim these truths and, if necessary, stand even against the institutional church when it contradicts Scripture in these areas. The debate is, if you like, all about Scripture and church authority. And this is the burden of Professor Beckwith's fourth point: given that there is a certain equivocal nature to the Catholic-Protestant debate on justification, better to back the church with historical and theological continuity with the first generations of Christians that followed Christ's Apostles. I have said enough already to indicate that I think this statement involves a romantic view of both the early church and the contemporary Catholic Church; more importantly, it rests upon notions of church authority and scriptural perspicuity and sufficiency, as well as the right and ability of the individual to read and learn from Scripture. Professor Beckwith has clearly come to repudiate basic Protestant positions in this area.

Given this, Professor Beckwith is absolutely right to have rejoined the Church of his youth. Not to have done so would presumably have been to go against his conscience. Yet, I would fire one shot across the bows at this point: while the issue of authority is too complicated to engage in a satisfactory way here, it is important to say that, for all of the crowing over the chaos in Protestantism by various Catholic ex-Protestants, I know of no more practically flexible and ultimately meaningless notion of authority than that which has historically been practiced by the papacy. Protestantism's chaos may be more evident at an institutional level; but maybe that just makes it more honest about its condition. I do not say that in order to be rude (though it may well not seem too polite!) but simply to point to what is for many Protestants the obvious elephant in the Catholic room.

A few years back, a good friend of mine, Dr Ray Van Neste of Union University, TN, did a survey of various scholars, asking if they could sign the ETS doctrinal statement. At least one leading Catholic wrote back to say yes—and the only reason why any Protestant could was because the Catholic Church had first defined these basic doctrines! Whether Professor Beckwith can legitimately remain a member of ETS is for others to decide. I am not a member any more. Ironically, I let my own membership lapse two years ago and joined the North American Patristic Society. My reason: there are now so many postmodern, open theist types in ETS (who can, I think, sign the doctrinal statement with integrity, so minimally orthodox and inadequate as a Christian statement it is) that I decided it was bizarre to remain a member of a group with many of whose members I had less in common than I do with good, confessionally Catholic friends. I resolved instead to use my money to learn more about the early church fathers from which later Christianity, both Catholic and Protestant, developed. Frankly, the NAPS is better value for money; and, believe it or not, patristic reading has persuaded me to stick with Geneva, rather than head to Rome.

THE THEATER OF THE ABSURD

One of the questions I have been asked with some frequency over the last month or so is why my contributions to the Reformation 21 blog tend to have something of a facetious edge to them. I am tempted to answer simply that that is the kind of person I am. If you want a bland blog, there are plenty of options out there, but, as Mariah Carey doesn't do stairs, I try my best not to do bland. Whether I'm successful or not is unclear, though the amount of hate mail is extremely encouraging in this regard: please keep sending it in; it means a lot to me and, judging by the adjectives alone, I know it means a lot to you too.

There is, however, more to it than the fact that I still have the mind of a seventeen-year-old schoolboy trapped inside an older but clearly no wiser body. It is that the whole blog phenomenon is inherently ridiculous; that the more serious it tries to be, the more absurd and pompous it becomes; and that I believe that if you can't beat the inevitable blogological deconstruction, you might as well join it, and that with relish. As the old Buddhist proverb says, "When faced with the inevitable, one must merely accept the inevitable."

Why is this the case? Well, let's backtrack a little. The right to free speech is one of the most treasured aspects of the American Constitution, enshrined as it is in the First Amendment. The freedom of the press is basic to this; yet we all know that the press is, by and large, the preserve of a wealthy elite. How many of us own newspapers or TV channels or have access to the contacts, the physical materials, and the distribution networks necessary to have our say in print or on the box? Very few. In theory we are all free to write, say, or read what we want; in practice, however, there are considerable constraints, ideological and material, personal and impersonal, on our capacity to realize this freedom to its fullest theoretical extent.

This is where the web makes things more than a little different. At least on the surface, the web allows anyone, anywhere to have their say. Of course, the reality is somewhat less than that: you need to have the money to fund your techno-habit; you need to have the educational training to use a computer; and you need to have the time to indulge in your passion. While blogs and chatrooms may be "changing the way the world is," I suspect that is rather more true for the children of stockbrokers in the American suburbs than for the nomads of northern Mongolia or the Berbers in the Moroccan desert. Nevertheless, it is clear that the capacity for greater participation in what we might call "media conversation" is now much greater, and much more instantaneous, than was ever possible with print or television.

What this increased freedom has arguably brought in its wake is a radical democratization of knowledge. Whereas in the past the availability of knowledge and the opportunity to participate in the various institutions and conversations surrounding knowledge was limited, now those limitations have been decidedly weakened. On one level, this is to be welcomed. Frankly, if I depended on the American news media to tell me what is going on anywhere outside of, well, umm, Philadelphia and its immediate suburbs, then I'd be lost, doomed to assuming that the Eagles catastrophic showing in the NFL this year has indeed been greeted with universal disappointment, from Chestnut Hill to Samarkand. Thanks to the web, however, I can still find out each day what goes on back in the old country, from proper sports, like rugby, to politics, arts, and entertainment. And the web potentially empowers groups who might otherwise find it hard to speak out—a little like the underground presses in Eastern Europe which played so signal a role in weakening the Iron Curtain during the seventies and eighties.

Yet even as this increasing freedom is to be welcomed, it is not without inherent problems. In the past, if I wanted to tell you my views on subatomic physics, the best an idiot like myself could have done was to self-publish a book on the subject; and as soon as bookstore managers and journal editors noticed that the book was published by the "Carl R. Trueman Center for Really Very Complicated Scientific Inquiry," no mainstream bookshop would stock it and no reputable organ would review it. These days, however, I could simply start my own web page or blog, and somebody out there—probably a bunch of my own besotted but unqualified and incompetent disciples—would take it seriously, flag up my works, surround my blogs and articles with praise, and make me look like a credible player in the internet world of subatomic research. Credible, that is, to anyone who took the web at face value and did not know anything about the subject or my own lack of any qualifications in the relevant field.

The problem is this: the free access to public exposure which the web provides has facilitated what appears to be a dangerous confusion of categories, that of the right to speak with the right to be heard. Now, as noted above, everyone in America, from Larry Flynt to James Dobson, from Jesse Jackson to David Duke, has a constitutionally enshrined right to speak; and as I am, in political terms, a leftish, libertarianish type of person, I would defend their right so to do; but I would deny that they each have an equal right to be heard. Frankly, the likes of Flynt and Duke sicken me to the pit of my stomach; they can say what they like, but I am not going to bother listening; and the Constitution does not require that I do so.

This is where the democratization of knowledge which the web has fueled is so damaging. Now anybody can spout on anything and find an audience, no matter how hateful or inept or ignorant they are. After all, cyberpsace dissolves the difference between a large, credible denomination, say The Presbyterian Church in America, and some survivalist nutcase out west who gathers with his wife and kids every Sunday and has a web page entitled "The Presbyterian Church in America (Reconstituted)." In web-world, both apparently have an equally legitimate existence and an equally legitimate right to be heard. On a more prosaic, and less harmful level, web pages and blogs allow any Tom, Dick, or Harriet, regardless of qualification, to hold forth on just about anything. And this is where it all gets so incredibly messy and even, in the technical sense, deconstructive.

A couple of recent examples which have been brought to my attention might help to illuminate the problem. One was a blogsite which railed against "self-appointed watchdogs" who do nothing but offer negative criticism of others. Well I never. An attack on negative, self-appointed watchdogs launched by—umm—a negative, self-appointed watchdog. Yet the apparent absurdity of the situation was entirely lost on the blogmeister who was engaged in this activity, oblivious to the obvious contradictions of his activity and attitude. It seems that where the web is concerned, negativity and self-appointment are in the eyes of the beholder. In this case, blogic aced logic, and the result was most unfortunate.

Then there was the case of a young guy who wanted to engage in e-mail banter about something I'd written. What fascinated me was the way this person referred to himself at one point in our exchange as a scholar. Yet he had no higher degree, no track record of publications which had passed muster with peers in the field. In fact, he's still a student, not yet even beginning a doctoral program. Indeed, he's a long way from possessing that most basic of academic union cards: a PhD. Now, I guess I'm old fashioned, but the category of scholar is one which should be reserved for those who have established themselves in their chosen field by actual scholarly achievement, not by simply talking a good game. This credibility is achieved by consistent, careful, and scholarly contributions to a field in terms of refereed publications which then enjoy currency among qualified peers outside the person's immediate circle of epigonous friends. Above all, "scholar" is a title that one never, ever applies to oneself. Yet here was this junior denizen of the web calling himself a "scholar," a title at which even most of the distinguished academics with whom I am familiar would blush if it were to be applied to them. What on earth was going on? I can only assume that this chap had been tricked by the fact that he hangs round on blog pages with mutually affirming virtual friends all day into imagining that he was a real player in the serious scholarly world beyond the blogosphere, so to speak. Yet, one might quip in response that having a vote and visiting a polling station every four years does not make one a professional politician, let alone the Prime Minister or the President. Once again, blogic aced logic; and, once again, the result was most unfortunate.

To cut to the chase, the danger of the web is this: where everyone has a right to speak, everyone ends up thinking they have a right to be heard; and when everyone in general thinks they have a right to be heard, then you end up with a situation where nobody in particular is listened to.

Let's conclude by bringing the point home to the church: the danger of an uncritical attitude to the web and to blogging is that it comports very easily with the conversational model of theology which is now gaining currency among the advocates of advanced modernism (aka postmodernism) of the Western church situation, where "Thus saith the Lord" is being displaced by "Come in, God, me old pal. Let's have a cup of coffee and a chat." The absolute democratization of knowledge to which an uncritical attitude to blogging, etc leads is, after all, inimical to any hierarchical view of truth, and thoroughly comfortable with the "this is my truth now tell me yours" approach which is gaining ground even as I write.

So how do we go about combating this? Well, we cannot abandon web-based media, so we should not try. Yet it seems to me the only way to avoid being co-opted into the pompous and arrogant numptiness of a world where students claim to be scholars and pit-bulls genuinely lament the unacceptable aggression of poodles is to do one of two things. We could make sure that the stuff we read in the virtual world is backed up by achievements out there in the real world. If a blogmeister is a bishop in the Catholic Church or has been moderator of a Presbyterian denomination or has a string of peer-reviewed publications in a given field, the term "self-appointed" is somewhat different when applied to that person than to some kid with an appetite for self-publicity and a networked computer in his bedroom. The latter certainly has a right to speak; but the former has actually earned the right to be heard.

Or you could try another way, what we might call the "Samuel Beckett" option: face this theater of the absurd head-on; join in with the other nobodies pretending to be somebodies; laugh at your own ridiculous complicity in this nonsense; expose the systemic contradictions for all they are worth; mock the blogworld for all of its inane self-importance; and in so doing try in some small way to subvert the system from the inside. It may not ultimately work; but you will have fun in the process.

2.11

LEADERSHIP, HOLY MEN, AND LESSONS FROM AUGUSTINE

The sad incident of the fall of the church leader Ted Haggard through public exposure of a relationship with a homosexual prostitute has provoked a variety of responses, including a number of posts on the blog attached to Reformation 21.[1] Most are predictable, and most are valid to some degree, whether they criticize Haggard for his hypocrisy or use him as an example of the power of sin that lies crouching at the door of all human beings, even—or perhaps especially—believers.

One response I have not noted, however, is the evidence that the Haggard case gives of the importance of studying patristic church history in order to gain understanding of the present. Of course, given the pain and trauma caused to his family by his actions, and the disappointment which many of those who trusted him must feel, this is hardly surprising: the thought that the discipline of studying the dry and dusty tomes of church history, let alone of ancient church history, might have something to offer at this juncture is probably not

---

[1] Ted Haggard, megachurch pastor and leader of the National Association of Evangelicals, resigned all his leadership positions in the wake of this scandal in November, 2006.

uppermost in the popular imagination. Nevertheless, I would like to suggest three ways in which the study of certain aspects of the ancient church can help us to understand in more detail what has gone on in this case.

At this point, some may simply respond by saying, "Look, the guy's a sinner; leaders have greater opportunity for sin, they aspire to the heights, and thus they fall more dramatically when they are caught doing something wrong. Do we need to dwell any further on the matter?" All that is undoubtedly true; but, as a historian, I would suggest that the more universal the reason given for a particular occurrence, the less satisfying the explanation tends to be. For example, if someone was to ask me why the Twin Towers fell down on September 11, 2001, and I were to reply that it was because of the laws of gravity, my explanation would be impeccable and true; yet at the same time it would also clearly be very inadequate, historically incomplete, and of little help in trying to prevent similar events occurring in the future. In much the same way, the response that Haggard fell because of sin is true; but this explanation is too general to be anywhere near satisfying and it offers no possibility of learning lessons for the future.

The three concepts connected to the study of the early church which I would suggest are key to developing a more profound and satisfying grasp of the Haggard situation are these: Donatism; the role and function of the Holy Man; and the Augustinian insight into sin as self-love which finds its fulfillment purely in itself.

DONATISM

As to the first, Donatism, I do not wish to expend much time as the point is fairly prosaic: the power of the gospel message is not a function of the moral probity of the preacher. If it were not so, who then could be saved? This was part of the point made in the Donatist controversies of the fourth and fifth centuries, where the question of what to do with those who lapsed in times of persecution became critical. The basic argument of Augustine and others was that the church is not dependent for its existence and authority on the moral fiber of her leaders. Not at all. The Word is powerful because it is God's Word, accompanied and applied by his Spirit. When a leader falls, it is disappointing; it hurts family; it discourages those who may have invested much in that person; but it no more necessarily invalidates the message they preached than their previously blameless character validated it. Did they preach God's Word? That is the only key question to ask on this point. Haggard has hurt his family and disappointed his church; but to the extent that he preached the Word (and I confess to being unfamiliar with his ministry), then that will stand the test of time.

THE HOLY MAN

The second aspect of patristic study which is helpful in this context is the notion of the Holy Man. Holy Men were individuals who chose lives of personal asceticism and self-denial and built up tremendous popular following in the fourth century and beyond. Often they lived at a little distance from population centers (but not so far that they could not be supplied with food and other necessities of life—church historians should never neglect the basic material necessities of life in their analyses, after all). Symeon Stylites, he of the "sitting up a pole for decades" fame, and who was later immortalized in a film by Spanish surrealist, Luis Bunuel, is perhaps one of the most well-known. As he grew holier, so his poles grew bigger; and after his death, the personality cult continued, with a church being built on the site of his last—and largest—podium.

More significant than the actual lives of these men were their literary Lives. Holy Men lived on beyond the grave in the accounts of their deeds which were passed from generation to generation; whether these were true accounts by some modern empirical standard or not is largely irrelevant; their teaching, their pattern of life, their values were communicated through the literary representations constructed by their biographers; and the most famous and influential of these "lives" was the Life of Anthony, an Egyptian Holy Man of the fourth century, whose deeds were recorded in an account traditionally ascribed to Athanasius, the great bishop of Alexandria and champion of Nicene orthodoxy.

Two things emerge from these accounts that have bearing on understanding the Haggard incident. The first is the clear development of an individual's authority based not upon their location in a system of institutional power but upon their charisma. Anthony and his ilk were lone rangers, answerable in the narratives of their lives to no one; they pursue their lonely course with vigor and remarkable success; they deal with temptation (invariably externalized in the form of demons, wealth, or women) by themselves in a form of spiritual mortal combat; and their actions are never questioned but simply the occasion for the increasing uncritical devotion of their growing band of followers. In the narratives, this is no problem, since the attacks on their souls are all external (doubters, demons, wild animals) and are always dispatched after a perfunctory, if vigorous, struggle. The accounts help to foster the image of invulnerable, gifted individuals who need answer to no one below God himself. Indeed, there are times in the texts when the language used of them is virtually christological, so exalted is their status. These were the superheroes, the demi-gods of the early church.

Now, the way in which the writers of these lives establish the superhero status of the Holy Men is interesting and pertinent to the Haggard case. They do this by continually underscoring the values and ideals to which the Holy Man generally conforms. This in itself is not surprising. What is surprising, however, is the nature of these values: these are often indistinguishable from those of the pagan world in which the Holy Man operates. For example, Holy Men exemplify a lifestyle of self-denying asceticism which was well-established in the ancient world as a virtue, and they also perform miracles which provide for the needs of those they meet (as well as supplying justification within the structure of the narratives of the Holy Men's social and economic usefulness). In other words, the kind of things at which a Holy Man excels are precisely those things which are already held in high esteem by the wider, pagan world within which he lives.

The connection between these two points — the charismatic actions of the Holy Men, and their connection to the values of pagan society — have a twofold effect: the power of the Holy Man resides in the fact that he can outdo the pagans at their own game; and in doing so, he makes himself an individual who stands out with the normal canons of routine, institutional accountability. The Holy Man's actions are not so much qualitatively as quantitatively different to those of the pagan opposition; his "apologetic" is thus an apologetic based on doing the same tasks better, on success pure and simple; and, as everyone knows, success is its own answer to criticism and weakens, if not abolishes, normal channels of accountability.

How does all this connect to Ted Haggard? Simple: he was a modern day Holy Man. OK, he did not live in the Utah desert on top of a great big pole; but asceticism was never the point even among the patristic Holy Men; the point was to outdo the pagans according to the pagans' own value scheme. And in a culture obsessed with success, with numbers, with social and political status and clout, Haggard had it all; and, crucially, he had more of it than most of the pagans.

For me, the most telling comment I heard in the whole scandal was a throwaway line in a television interview, filmed before the storm broke as part of a documentary. Here Haggard declared that survey after survey indicated that evangelical Christians had the best sex lives. Now, of course, this rather inane comment seems sadly ironic; and the media undoubtedly played on it simply to demonstrate the man's sad hypocrisy. Yet in so doing they actually missed the real significance of what Haggard was doing at this point and squandered the opportunity for a really clever, profound analysis of the comment by using it to get a cheap, banal snigger. In fact, Haggard's reference to the sexual superiority of evangelical love lives was a classic move which could have taken its cue from an ancient Holy Man narrative: Christianity is much better at all of the things which paganism holds dear. You pagans got sex? Well, we got it better! Once again,

Haggard played the game of besting the pagans even on that ground which they themselves consider most holy.

The net result of all this is, of course, that Holy Men like Haggard are effectively rendered unaccountable to anyone: the size and commitment of his congregation, like the multitude gathered around Symeon on his pole or Anthony in the desert, confirmed his charismata and validated his success; and success not only breeds success, but also immunizes against criticism. Indeed, in such a context, criticism must always appear to be small-minded, nasty, and envious. After all, who is going to hold accountable or doubt the integrity of a man who seems to be outgunning the pagans with Christian weaponry at the very points where those same pagans place most of their pride? When you pack your church to the gunwales, enjoy afternoon tea at the White House, and hobnob with George W, you really do stand above the ordinary herd.

SELF-LOVE AS AN END IN ITSELF

This leads me to the third aspect of the Haggard case upon which the study of the early church can shed light. It is well-known that Augustine regarded the essence of sin as the love of self as an end in itself. While human beings were designed to love, they were really intended to love God in and for himself, and to love themselves and others primarily as a means to that ultimate, unconditional love of God. The tragedy of fallen humanity is that men and women love themselves and that such love is regarded as an end in itself. Thus, we might say that the essence of sin is for humans to place themselves where God should be—in the place of that which is to be loved.

When we examine a case such as that of Ted Haggard, one of the obvious points to make is that Haggard was a Christian leader; and the received wisdom is that leaders have greater temptations and greater opportunities to sin. Such is certainly the case; but I think there is more to sin in leadership than simply the fact that leaders have greater scope for moral deviancy.

Leaders are interesting creatures in whatever field they happen to be. For a start, they carry more responsibility, take more heat, and endure more hits than those who are not leaders. The marketplace recognizes this by generally giving better relative pay to those who hold such positions of responsibility in particular spheres: the bank manager earns more than the cashier; the police commissioner than the copper on the beat; the Prime Minister than the newly minted backbencher. In each case it is because the burden of responsibility is that much greater for the former than for the latter.

Given this, one way of approaching sin in leadership might be to emphasize the fact that the leader who routinely shoulders more responsibility might well get into the habit of cutting himself or herself more slack when it comes to the perks and fringe benefits which come his or her way. "I take more grief, therefore I should treat myself to a little bit more of the good life than others" the argument might go; and one could certainly cast such an argument in terms of self-love and see in it the proverbial slippery slope which might, if left unchecked, lead to personal moral chaos. Today, I treat myself to the extra glass of wine at lunch; tomorrow I help myself to an underling's spouse.

There is certainly some truth in this kind of argument; but I believe that Augustine's psychology of sin offers a more satisfying theological account. I would suggest that the key to understanding the sin of leaders lies in the quasi-godlike status of leaders themselves, a status which provides rich soil for the kind of self-deification which lies at the heart of sin.

Leaders are godlike within their spheres of authority: they make rules; they enforce rules; they command people to do things and these people obey or face the consequences. On this level, leadership is highly seductive, playing to the innate tendency in all fallen human beings to exalt themselves as God. Put bluntly, power in the human sphere serves only to confirm the lie that the self-loving human heart tells itself: *you are god; you* are the object which *you* are to love in order to find *your* true being and fulfillment.

We can now take this point a stage further: in this context, that of the godlike aspirations of leadership, sin becomes incredibly attractive. In the *Confessions*, Augustine makes it clear in relation to a trivial act of the youthful crime of stealing some pears from a neighbor's tree. It was not the pears themselves, he argues, that made the crime attractive—he remembers that he had better pears in his own garden—but the act of transgression. He liked *breaking the rules* much more than he liked the taste of the pears; and we might gloss this by saying that he liked breaking the rules because, in breaking the rules he effectively declared himself to be god, the one who makes up his own rules and thus stands above the law. When we connect this to leadership, it is easy to see why the culture of leadership is one in which sin is not simply a danger because of the greater opportunities which leadership offers; it is also a danger because the culture of leadership is one where making the rules and enforcing them as and when desired is part and parcel of how the leader operates. In his or her respective field, the leader has a sweeter, deeper, more intoxicating taste of a pseudo-divine freedom than that available to the ordinary person in the street, and given the self-directed nature of fallen humanity, it is inevitable that outwith the grace of God the results will be disastrous.

Self-love which is an end in itself is, of course, narcissism; and it is often noted how many narcissists make it to the top in their respective fields, driven by the need to feed their own self-image, to satiate, as Augustine might say, the insatiable: they love themselves, and that love, because it does not terminate on the infinite God, can never satisfy; and so it serves only to drive them on to greater heights of self-love, evidenced in everyday life by massive overachievement. Hence, so the received wisdom goes, they tend to rise to the top.

In addition, narcissists' delusions of deity lead them to routinely break the rules themselves while imposing these rules with a ruthless efficiency on those under them. After all, narcissists thinks they are gods; and just as gods stand above their own laws, so they demand absolute obedience from those lesser beings who stand below them. As Augustine might have put it, everyone else becomes something the individual merely *uses* to achieve the ends of his or her own self-love, instruments kept in their place by subjugation to the law from which the narcissist considers himself to be free because of his or her superiority. Perhaps it is therefore not insignificant that a hallmark of Haggard's public presence was his outspoken opposition to gay marriage; given the nature of his fall, it is difficult not to be reminded of this classic narcissistic pattern of rigidly demanding obedience from others on a point where one indulges oneself routinely in transgression.

Given this tendency, the received wisdom—that narcissists tend to rise to the top—needs perhaps to be modified. The godlike pretensions of the narcissist and the godlike analogies of the nature of leadership itself are perhaps symbiotic, feeding off each other. Perhaps it is not narcissists who make leadership material, but leadership which capitalizes on human weaknesses and feeds and strengthens those tendencies which make individuals into narcissists. Given this, it is not surprising to see leaders fall frequently and spectacularly. It is not simply that leaders have greater opportunities to sin; it is that the very nature of leadership will seduce all but the most careful into believing that they are little gods, that they make the rules, and that they can get away with anything. Surround these leaders with crowds of uncritically adoring supporters and you have the perfect storm: self-deception followed by self-destruction are, humanly speaking, almost unavoidable.

It is perhaps worth noting at this point, almost as an aside, that one refreshing factor in the Haggard case was the way in which his followers dealt with him firmly and decisively. The self-love of the leader is so often paralleled by the self-love of the followers; and it is always amazing to see for how long, and with what vehemence, the followers of morally discredited and bankrupt leaders remain committed to their former masters. It seems the mutual ego-stroking of leader and disciple often pays dividends for the former when the toothpaste finally comes out of the tube; as the Holy Man gives his followers vicarious charismata and importance during the good times, so the effect seems to last long after the grace has well and truly departed.

This brings me to my final Augustinian take on the Haggard affair: for Augustine, sexual union is the classic locus of self-love. This is why he believes that original sin is transmitted: even the very act of conception is perverted by self-love and thus the products of that union are themselves damaged from conception. Indeed, in Augustine's thought, the separation of sexual union from procreation is an example of self-love as an end in itself in action. Once the purpose of sexual union terminates on pleasure rather than on reproduction, the game is up as far as virtuous sex goes. On this issue, I disagree with Augustine and find, for example, Gilbert Meilaender's recent defense of sexual intercourse for purposes other than the reproductive to be persuasive. Nevertheless, once sexual union is divorced from the context of marriage, I believe that the Augustinian critique is basically sound: sex for ends other than the reproductive or the strengthening and nourishing of the marriage bond ends up as sex for self-serving purposes, whether personal physical pleasure, personal power, or whatever.

Given this, the fact that sexual sin is so often the Achilles heel of leaders, even Christian leaders, is not surprising. After all, one would expect those who are drowning in self-love and thus self-deception regarding their status as little gods to be prone to give expression to that in their actions; and surely the ultimate expression of this is sex purely motivated by personal satisfaction. Even mistresses do not provide this opportunity for total self-directed self-love, as the lover's bond to the mistress might still involve some level of personal emotional commitment and hold open the possibility of procreation and family life; but prostitutes, perhaps especially gay prostitutes, provide precisely such a nihilistic outlet for sexual activity where the focus is surely directed entirely at transgressive, anarchic behavior which places self-satisfaction and personal fulfillment right at the center, any emotional or reproductive needs of the partner being totally excluded from the picture.

CONCLUSION

To summarize the arguments so far: leaders such as Ted Haggard are akin to the Holy Men of the early church. They are individuals of great charisma who symbolize the superiority of Christianity by outdoing the pagans in terms of the measures of success within the wider society; and such culturally acceptable success lifts them above criticism, giving them a quasi-godlike status. In addition, there is a certain parallel between the nature of human leadership in general as that which involves power and the nature of human sin as the transgression of God's law. Throw into the mix crowds of adoring followers and a culture which judges success by numbers, wealth, access to the media, and to the great and the good in Washington or elsewhere, and you have a situation where the capacity for human self-love and self-deception can potentially spiral out of control. That this so often finds expressing in sexual encounters of the most transgressive nature should be no surprise, for such activity is human self-love in its most unadulterated form.

Where does this lead us? I close with just three points:

1. Ancient church history, far from being a matter of only antiquarian interest, can, when done with a properly critical eye, provide us with categories which allow us to analyze events in the present at a depth to which we might not otherwise have access. To respond to incidents like those involving Ted Haggard with responses which simply point to the fact that he is a sinner, or that his actions are foolish, is legitimate; but it does not really allow us to probe the psychology of leadership and the peculiar problems such leadership brings within a culture such as ours.

2. Leadership is a potentially lethal position. Those who are leaders are not simply given more opportunities to sin; they actually inhabit a place which positively fosters the kind of self-deception which lies at the very heart of what sin is. If routine sin allows us, even momentarily, to think that we are gods, then the leader lives in a world where that potential image of self can be reinforced again and again by power and by the adulation and/or obedience of others. Perhaps the people we need to lead us, whom we can really trust, are, first and foremost, those who do not want to be leaders but have the role thrust upon them.

Scripture tells us, of course, that it is a good and noble thing to desire to be a leader; but perhaps we need to pay careful attention to how someone desires to be a leader, and how responsible they have proved in the small things of life before we automatically assume that the desire to be a leader actually confirms the call to leadership.

3. Accountability is thus crucial in leadership. Choice of advisors and confidantes is critical. The tragedy of Haggard and of others like him is that they did not put into place the right men and women before the problem developed. If you want to avoid personal moral disaster as a Christian, you need to establish mechanisms of accountability before you think you have any problem; and for leaders this is even more imperative. Being surrounded by yes-men and lackeys might stroke the self-image; but it will do nothing to prevent self-destruction.

And I learned all this from critical reflection on texts written over 1,500 years ago.

2.12

ESCAPING VANITY FAIR

A WORD OF ENCOURAGEMENT

FROM NIETZSCHE

The domestication of radical ideas is a well-known phenomenon to anyone who has ever spent time reflecting on history. Browsing in "Borders" recently, I found Marx's *Communist Manifesto* on one of the shelves. This was not in itself surprising; but what was startling was the fact that I could buy it in no less than five different editions. Same book, same text, but five different covers. This was irony in action: the basic anti-capitalist, anti-consumerist war-cry available in so many convenient editions. Why? Because, of course, Marx sells; his book has become a commodity; and the variety of editions speak of the way in which consumerism has overcome and internalized his critique, turning it from a passionate attack and prediction of its doom into one more item on the shelf, to be packaged and marketed, repackaged and remarketed. What will happen next? Can we expect this secular scripture to go the way of more sacred texts, with editions of the *Manifesto* for singles, young marrieds, teenagers, small groups, CEOs, vegetarians, young women, old men, and slimmers? If it can be sold, sooner or later it will be done.

Similar domestication happens also with individuals who embody certain radical stands: Che Guevara is perhaps the archetypal example of this in the last fifty years. In life he was a disciplined and driven revolutionary, a ruthless and cold-blooded killer, and one who had the reputation of being somewhat dour, with little time for anything or anyone unconnected to the ultimate goal of socialist revolution. In death, however, he became almost immediately an icon of a hedonistic sixties youth protest movement which had little interest in discipline or self-denial or ruthless execution of enemies for that matter; and, in the years since 1967, he has become little more than a marketing logo, a symbol and a facilitator of the capitalism he despised. Divorced from its original context, his messianic face, clad in guerrilla garb, stares portentously from a myriad of teeshirts, coffee mugs, beer bottles, and designer handbags.

If there is real and amusing irony in the domestication of Marx and Che, then the same kind of principles can be seen to apply to the world of music. Here, the story is complicated by the fact that the music of, say, Bob Dylan or The Rolling Stones or Bruce Springsteen was always parasitic upon the system which it was attacking: all such rebels depended upon record companies with the marketing power and savvy to produce and promote their products; all depended upon people with money to buy them. Thus, at the very outset, one could almost have predicted that, sooner or later, middle-aged, middle-class theology professors would be listening to The Clash's great anthem "London Calling" as they drove to work in the morning. In the dialectic of protest and commerce, protest lost, content proved less important than aesthetics, and rock became one more sellable commodity of the commercial establishment.

The Christian religion too is no stranger to such domestication. A first-rate example would be the blond and blue-eyed Jesus beloved by so many children's Bible illustrators and cheesy Christian artists of earlier generations. Perhaps it was relatively harmless to portray the Lord in a children's Bible as looking like Benny (or was it Bjorn?), the ABBA keyboard player; but when we remember that the blond and blue-eyed Messiah was also the object of the *forgotten* quest for the historical Jesus—that pursued by anti-Semitic German scholars between the Wars—it is clear that such domestication is not always so trivial.

Of course, scholars from Adolf Schlatter to N. T. Wright have been debunking this kind of rubbish for quite some time now; but, in all of the effort to free the Bible from domesticated categories, it is sometimes forgotten that the taming of Christianity is not limited to the biblical text. For example, once theological education became competitive big business, the marketing of it turned into something well beyond the simple description to prospective students of what goes on at a seminary or a college. There is a complex relationship between traditional curricula, the demands of the church, the expectations of the students, and the ability of the marketplace itself not simply to satisfy needs but also to create needs and open up new markets. The implications of theology as commodity have not yet been self-consciously addressed by educational institutions; and, given the nature of the free market as something of a sacred cow in current Western thinking, such questions are unlikely to be pressed in the foreseeable future.

Yet education is not the only object of domestication in religious culture. Take the writer C. S. Lewis, for example. As I understand him, he was not an evangelical and never claimed to be an evangelical. Indeed, I suspect that, as a die-hard patrician Anglican, he would have been less than pleased with the idea of becoming the patron saint of a religion with such a populist and democratized ethos. Yet he has developed an almost cult-like status within the evangelical culture of North America. What are we to make of this? Well, I always tell students that the first question to ask about any historical action is this: who makes money out of the deal? And there is no doubt that Lewis's writings represent a solid source of revenue for those publishing and selling religious books, and that much of the market share is represented by evangelicals.

The market for Lewis among evangelicals, however, cannot be reduced to a publisher's sales pitch: whatever some of the more hardline members of the Frankfurt School might have argued, consumers are not just hapless dupes of the system;

the relationship between producer and consumer is more complex than that; and thus the market for Lewis must find some foothold within American evangelical culture itself. I would suggest three internal causes which have facilitated his marketability—and this is not an exclusive list, merely a suggestive one. First, he advocates a mere Christianity which is very appealing to the transdenominational spirit of American evangelicalism, particularly in the aestheticized world of postmodernism. Second, his books are well-written and accessible, a combination difficult to find in most evangelical writing (Catholics have Chesterton, Waugh, and Greene, to name but three; we have Jenkins and La Hay...). And third— and perhaps most crucial—modern American culture finds intellectual disagreement to be something best understood by using the categories of moral antithesis. This is surely part of the reason why the language of political campaigning in the US has so little to do with actual policies and so much to do with assessments of character and with exercises in simplistic moral sloganeering. If someone disagrees with me on how the local garbage collection should be financed, it is not simply that the two of us differ over how tax should be levied and disbursed. It is surely a certain sign that he probably beats his wife, was rude to his mother, and has a frequent and irresistible urge to push old ladies under the wheels of oncoming trains—all of which render him incapable of organizing garbage collection. Thus, a Christian thinker like Lewis presents a problem to evangelicals, given his views on issues such as purgatory and the atonement. But he still offers us certain things that are attractive—mere Christianity, good writing, etc, things that we want to be able to appreciate and use. So what is to be done? Simply this: he needs to be turned into one of us so that we can feel comfortable with him. And, as an aside, one might add that it is quite useful that he's dead at this point, as his reputation, as well as his literary remains, are no longer his to possess and define. A little bit like Mormon baptism of the dead.

Lewis is not the only candidate for a makeover, however. In many ways a more interesting example of domestication is provided by John Bunyan's *Pilgrim's Progress*. This is surely one of those books which enjoys almost universal appeal among Christians across the denominational boundaries for the profound simplicity of its narration of the Christian life through allegory. Yet the book's simplicity is deceptive, and its reception into the canon of universal Christian classics should actually be very surprising to all who read it. For a start, the picture it paints of the Pope, sitting gibbering in a cave while gnawing on the bloody bones of the martyrs, would have led one to expect that its appeal within modern ecumenical evangelical circles (not to mention those of Roman Catholics!) might be somewhat limited. Bunyan was, after all, part of a Protestant culture which saw Rome as an agency of the Devil and which was even more adept at finding Jesuits under the stairs than Joseph McCarthy was at finding reds under beds.

Yet Bunyan's ferocious critique is not confined simply to the doctrinal and ecclesiastical divisions of his day. Outrage at social and economic injustice permeates the work as well. Bunyan was, after all, a poor man, a tinker, a mender of pots and pans, a man of no consequence in an increasingly commercial world. Read *Pilgrim's Progress* again and notice how his lowly status and his fear of the wealthy and the men of commerce seethes within the narrative. Who is Giant Despair? A thuggish landowner. Where are the pilgrims most notably ill-treated, even to the point of martyrdom for the one? Vanity Fair, a scene of commerce and decadence. And how many times are the scoundrels in the narratives also described as gentlemen? The terms are virtually interchangeable. Any suggestive patterns emerging? No reasonably thoughtful seventeenth-century reader would have missed the brutal polemic against the wealthy and the establishment. Truth be told, Bunyan's great Puritan classic is not simply a statement of radical theology; it is also an expression of radical politics, an historical action which cannot be properly understood in isolation from the turbulent milieu of a resurgent monarchy, a failed Puritan republicanism, the oppression of the poor, and the fear of a Catholic political and religious renaissance. A work of deep piety it surely is; but to read it and to fail to understand its subversively stated social, political, and ecclesiastical radicalism is to domesticate it and to miss much of its critical value. It is, to put it bluntly, to tame the tinker.

These readings of Lewis and Bunyan represent two different but related phenomena. For Lewis, as I say, it seems to be by and large a sales ruse which accommodates him to the limits of the potential market: evangelicals, because they define themselves doctrinally at some level, even if only minimally, struggle with those with whom they disagree ("Are they really Christian if they do/don't believe in x?"), a trait compounded by American cultural predispositions; thus, if he is to sell well, Lewis must be packaged and pitched as an evangelical. For Bunyan, it is more of the problem of a changed textual context: the twenty-first century Christian world is simply so different to that of seventeenth-century England that much of Bunyan's original intent is lost in transmission. The tinker travels through time and is tamed by that very process.

The relationship between the two phenomena lies in the fact that both demonstrate the readiness of human beings to read themselves into texts and thus to avoid the challenges that such texts offer to us. The real loss in the domestication of Lewis and Bunyan, in the reduction of them to the dimensions of a generic Christian piety, is the loss of the past as a critical foundation for reflection and self-examination. A history which panders to the marketplace or to boundaries set by the expectations of the modern audience becomes little more than a projection of contemporary concerns. It may use the idioms of history—the past tense and the language of hallowed tradition—but it is no history at all. It destroys the real usefulness of these men by imperiously imposing the present upon them, by demanding that they be like us, the customers; and it serves only to insulate us from criticism and to reinforce our own belief in our own rectitude. By contrast, I would argue that Lewis, Bunyan, and all great theological voices speak importantly at precisely those points where they least fit with my evangelical expectations, because it is at those points that they force me to think most carefully about who I am, where I am, what I believe, and why I believe it. Yet such critique is something which is very difficult to maintain in a world where market forces are the unseen and undetected powers that shape so much of reality, from institutions of education to churches to individual tastes. Critical voices which the market cannot internalize appeal neither to the godlike market forces of consumerism nor to the self-worshiping tendency of my own mind; but as a Christian I am surely required to fight against all idolatries, external and internal.

How can this be done? I would argue that the need of the hour is for the development of a proper evangelical critical theory, or, perhaps better, an evangelical self-critical theory. Not one which simply develops an arcane technical language designed to impress the world with the Gnostic sophistication of its advocates, as seems to be the case with some of the hermeneutical overload of recent years—such is simply a new elitism; nor one which simply parrots the latest cultural clichés in a sad attempt to appear hip and trendy like some beer-bellied middle-aged academic with a ponytail and a "Legalise Pot" teeshirt; least of all one that terminates simply in clever but sneering analysis that merely describes the world as it is. No. We need a critical theory that seeks to change the world by challenging the world—including the world of evangelicals—in its market-driven, all, consuming consumerist idolatries.

Given the way in which evangelical culture in America is so deeply embedded in the systems, practices, and aspirations of American culture in general—from its colleges and seminaries to its publishing houses to its relentless vision of "big is best" to its personality cults of celebrity theologians to its mega-ministries to its amazing ability to transform anyone, even the patrician Anglican C. S. Lewis and the radical tinker John Bunyan—into friendly evangelical allies, the outlook is not bright. To put it bluntly, we live in Vanity Fair, and we seem to be quite happy there. But recognizing the problem is surely the first part of the solution, and doing so, while awesome and terrifying on one level, should not be unduly discouraging to us. To quote Nietzsche, that which does not destroy me makes me stronger.

2.13

DEATH,
THE FINAL BOUNDARY

It is arguable that the last hundred years have witnessed an interesting reversal in Western society, where the great taboo of the Victorian era and the great obsession of the same period have dramatically switched places. The great taboo for Victorians was, of course, sex. Human beings all depend on sex—ignoring *in vitro* fertilization for a moment, we are each living proof of an act of sexual intercourse; yet the Victorians proved remarkably adept at keeping the whole matter well and truly out of the public eye. Death, however, was everywhere, from the elaborate funeral rituals and grotesque mausoleums, to the great works of art and literature. Sex the taboo; death the obsession.

Today, the roles are somewhat reversed. Sex is everywhere. I cannot even switch on my television at breakfast time without being confronted with some news story or interview which brings a blush to my wife's cheeks and sees me scrambling for the off-switch before my children receive an unexpected lesson in the latest sexual gossip. Watching commercials is no better: it seems that the notion that sex sells is now universally applied to anything which needs marketing, from paper clips to sports cars. But death—that's a different story. Death is something most of us try to avoid.

Western society has generated various means by which thinking about death can be avoided. On one level, there are the trivial quirks of language: for example, if someone is plucked from a flaming building or a sinking ship, we talk of a *life being saved* not of a *death being postponed*. The former seems somehow more acceptable, though the latter is arguably more accurate. Then there is the veritable industry in anti-ageing products, which I have noted in this column before (and confessed to having purchased for my wife). More subtly, there is the trivialization of death in the various movies, TV shows, and even newscasts, where it is variously turned into a surreal piece of cartoonish entertainment, an object of saccharine sentimentality, or simply sanitized in a way that can be addressed very briefly and then forgotten about before turning to the weather forecast, or the sports' results. On the news, it's something that happens to other people in far-off countries, or neighborhoods which few of us frequent. That is why the killing of one white man in the suburbs often precipitates more fear and panic about the end of civilization than the death of thousands in famines abroad or even the daily murder of numerous Hispanics and African-Americans just five miles down the road. When it happens to "us," we can't sanitize it quite as easily.

Yet for all these mechanisms for sanitizing and neutralizing death, death is still stubbornly universal. On the surface it is, after being born, the most natural thing in the world—it would seem certain that everybody, man, woman, and child, will one day die. This raises the question of why death is so traumatic: if it is natural, why do I still feel pain, so many years on, when I think of the last time I saw my beloved grandfather alive, knowing he had only hours to live? Why is it a shattering experience to lose a parent, or a sibling, or a friend, or, perhaps most nightmarish of all, a child to the last great enemy? If it's natural, why does death wreak such havoc upon us? And why do we go to such lengths to ignore it, to sentimentalize it, or to fictionalize it?

Several thoughts occur to me in this context. Death is not, of course, natural. It is an intrusion into the created realm. When God created man, the only thing that was not good was the fact that he was alone, and woman was thus created to be his companion. There was no sign of death; rather, death intruded into creation as a result of humanity's disobedience and is thus not part of the natural created structure of reality. Wittgenstein somewhere describes death rather memorably as not being an event in life, but a boundary; and the Christian can, I think, say amen to that, with the necessary addition that it is a boundary *which should not be there*. It is not natural, and thus we should not expect it to bring anything other than chaos and trauma in its wake.

Further, death is total. One can catch a cold and get well again; one can get AIDS and be kept alive now for many years; one can even have a cardiac arrest and still be revived. But death, when all the vital organs shut down, is complete and total. There is no return. I live in a land far from my parents and siblings; but I can get on a plane and be with them in less that ten hours. My grandparents are dead and buried. I can travel all over the world and meet thousands and thousands of people; but not one of them will be my grandfather or grandmother; they are gone; their death is total; they can no longer be found in the land of the living.

Yet as Christians there is that part of us that kicks in at this point: don't all things happen according to God's will? And if death happens according to God's will, what right have we to be angry and hurt by it? Does not the knowledge that God is in control render such feelings wrong?

Of course, the theology underlying this kind of claim is entirely correct. God is indeed in control. But does that mean that we are wrong to feel pain and hurt? Absolutely not. The darkness of death may well fall on each of us at the time and the place and in the manner in which God has decreed, but, as noted above, death is not natural; it is something which runs against the design of nature and it is therefore something which brings chaos and trauma into our lives. Further, the Bible does not just teach that all things happen within the compass of God's will; it also teaches that death is painful, and that feelings of anger, hurt, despair, and sympathy are not wrong. Just read the Psalms and see how the souls of the psalmists cry out in agony, and how those very words of agony are used by the Lord to form a substantial part of God's very own book of praise. Then think of Job who mourned and yet did not sin (Job 1:20-22), and even the Lord Jesus Christ himself who stood outside the tomb of his friend and wept (John 11:33-36). Sadness, deep sadness, and mourning in the face of death are not wrong: they are the result of being faced with a boundary which should not be there. If Thomas Hobbes could describe life as nasty and brutish, how much more does that description apply to death, the final boundary of that life?

But the unnatural nature of death is not the only reason why it hurts, and why we mourn when it happens. Human beings are not designed to live in isolation; we are made to live in relation with others. We are designed, first and foremost, to live in relation with God. Our fundamental identity is that of God's creatures. To understand myself correctly, I need to understand that I am created by God, in his image, and am utterly dependent upon him for all that I am and do. Yet there's much more to my identity than that. If it was not good for Adam to be alone, then it is clear that Adam was designed not simply to live in relation with God but also to find his full identity by existing in relation to another creature of the same kind. In other words, who I am is not an isolated individual. I am someone who stands in a complex web of relationships with others. Thus, when someone dies, I am reduced, I am damaged, I am changed. Once I had grandparents; now I am the man whose grandparents have gone; once a man was a father; now, tragically, he is no longer a father but the man whose child has died. In each case, those left behind are reduced, they are less than they once were; and that is painful. As John Donne so eloquently stated it: ask not for whom the bell tolls. It tolls for thee.

There is, however, one final reason why we find death so painful: the death of others is a mirror in which we see our own mortality reflected back to us. In facing the death of another, we are forced, however briefly, to face up to our own inevitable demise. Most of the time we can and do live our lives as if we are immortal, as if we are little gods, supreme potentates of the universe in which we live; but the death of another is a startling reminder that we are not divine, that there will be a final reckoning with death, that the boundary that should not be there for us will one day be only too present. Whether it is the passing of a distant acquaintance, whispering to us that we too shall perish, or the death of a close friend or loved one which seems to grab us violently by the throat and forces us to stare into the abyss of our own finitude—whatever it may be, as we witness death in others, we anticipate the day of our own demise.

So death is nasty, brutish, painful for a variety of reasons. How should we then as Christians respond to all this? Let me suggest three things:

First, it is quite all right to mourn, to feel agony and pain, even to taste the bitterness of a certain despair, in the face of death. The Psalms and the example of Christ himself surely leave us in no doubt about that. Despair, of course, can never be total for a Christian who looks to God for all things; but great, even overwhelming darkness can exist when we are faced with the reality of death. And if anyone asks, "How can I speak to God in such circumstances?" my advice is simple: if you lack the words yourself, then pray through the Psalms. For example, just read Psalm 88 and see how much despair, albeit set in the context of crying out to God in faith, grips the writer. You will find in the Psalms that there is not a single emotion which you feel which the Lord himself has not given us the words to express to him in prayer and praise. Learn to pray the Psalms in private, for there you find the resources to cope with the day of death and darkness. And I've said it before and I'll say it again: the neglect of the Psalter in public Christian worship lays the groundwork for pastoral disaster: it has the effect of shortchanging the brokenhearted when they come to God in the company of their brothers and sisters on the Lord's Day. Miserable Christians have every right, and indeed really must, express their misery to God in prayer and praise. To prevent them from doing so is an act of pastoral cruelty. And isn't it wonderful that we have such a God as the one who condescended in love and grace towards broken humanity to give us the Psalms for these very times of darkness? Then let's not neglect them; let's use them as much as we can, in private prayer and in public worship.

Second, let us never try to comfort a bereaved believer by simply telling them that the death of a loved one was all within the will of God. That is true, but if we stop there, we give only half the story and make ourselves vulnerable to accusations of pastoral cruelty. The other half of the Christian story when it comes to suffering and death is that we should feel with the hurting and the bereaved in their pain and loss, sympathizing, grieving, and mourning with them. Perhaps this involves speaking words of comfort, perhaps simply sitting with them in silence as they cry out in pain. But never let us selectively use our theology, however correct it may be, as an excuse to be less than human in the face of another's suffering.

Finally, let us never forget that the gospel is for Christians too. We need to hear the Word preached to us, whether from the pulpit on a Sunday or in conversation with other believers. If a brother or sister is mourning, then let us not simply tell them that the death of their loved one is all within the will of God; let us not even stop with simply feeling compassion and sympathy for them; let us also point them to the Lord Jesus Christ who rose from the dead. Death is an outrage, an illegitimate boundary; it is nasty and brutish; but the captain of our salvation has burst through that boundary and come out on the other side. He is risen from the grave; and in his resurrection we see that, though we live in a vale of tears and agony here and now, where death seems to hold all the trump cards, there is a day most certainly coming when we know that we too, and all the loved ones who have gone before us in Christ, will rise to be with Christ. His death was agonizing but it could not hold him; ours will no doubt be terrible and traumatic; but because of Christ, death will not hold us either.

2.14

A Dangerous Gift
for my Wife

Waiting for a flight to Philadelphia in Heathrow Terminal 4 recently, I engaged in my usual ritual: buying my children copies of the *Beano* and the *Dandy* comics, and some chocolate that tastes like real chocolate (seemingly illegal in the USA), and finding a present for my wife. A couple of years ago, I cracked the latter problem by discovering that she liked Gaultier perfume; but, having traveled so much, I have purchased it at a rate somewhat greater than her ability to use it and I was under instructions not to bring any more of the stuff home with me. Strange, that—I can't imagine ever thinking that, if the roles were reversed, my wife could ever buy me too much brandy or scotch or rock music. "Please, love, no more of that XO brandy; I've no more room in the drinks cabinet to keep yet another bottle...." To quote John Wayne, that'll be the day. But there you go—men are from Mars, women really are from Venus.

Anyway, finding myself in the classic male crisis situation of having to buy something nice for my wife but having no clue as to what to get her, I put into action a tried-and-tested strategy: I planted myself firmly in the cosmetics section of the World Traveller Duty Free Shop and adopted a facial expression which was half confusion, half outright panic. This ruse never fails: within moments, I was approached by one of the ladies who works in the shop and who is, presumably, trained to spot the presence of any married Neanderthal such as myself who is facing the "wife gift dilemma."

I explained my problem to her, how perfume would not cut it this time and how I desperately needed to find another form of spousal propitiation. She responded by asking a question cunningly designed, I believe, to diagnose the depths of my ignorance: "What kind of skin does she have?" she asked. "Well, it sort of covers her whole body and it's kind of, umm, whitish pink in color, I guess. Is that any good as an answer?" I responded, looking hopefully at the lady for signs that this was the kind of information she needed.

Having thus established that she was dealing with an extreme case of male incompetence and insensitivity, the lady then asked about my wife's age. "Thirty-nine," I answered. "Have you thought of anti-ageing cosmetics?" was the follow-up question. Anti-ageing cosmetics? "Do you think that's, err, wise? Wouldn't a gift like that have to be rather carefully stage-managed?" I asked somewhat hesitantly. I had visions of any box marked "anti-ageing" being as welcome a gift for my wife as one marked "emergency weight loss pills" or "excess facial hair remover." "That's all right, sir, no need to worry" the lady reassured me, "We don't actually use that phrase on the packet. And such products actually start for those aged thirty-five." Relief; problem solved; male ineptitude once again overcome by female omnicompetence.

On the flight back, I found myself reflecting on how the whole notion of an anti-ageing product is so typical of the Western world in which we live, a world which has made a veritable cult out of youth. Indeed, so many of our modern cultural fetishes speak so clearly of this obsession: fashion, sport, celebrity—all either pander to, or are in their very essence celebrations of, the young, the vibrant, the unwrinkly.

Why youth is to be so prized cannot, I suspect, be separated from such social (and, let's face it, economic) fetishes. Youth probably started its inexorable rise to importance with the development of production-based economies in the early modern era where the ability to produce was crucial—a point which was a bit of a downer for women past the age of childbearing and thus no longer capable of the most obvious contribution to economic productivity. This is certainly a factor in the disproportionate focus on older women exhibited by that most medieval-looking of early modern phenomena, the witch trial. Then, with the advent of consumption as the key factor driving Western economies, the opening up of easy credit, and the identification of youth and all things youthful as vast marketing opportunities, the triumph of the young and the beautiful was guaranteed. Even in societies that modernized without the obvious abandonment of feudal values, such as those in the Far East, youth is slowly coming into its own: on a recent trip to Korea I was struck by the awkward conflict between the typical Confucian veneration of age and the obviously booming—and somewhat anomalous—market for plastic surgery. Anyway, so much for the hard-nosed economic history of youth's importance.

Philosophically, however, we could look at the idolatry of youth in a different way. The obsession with youthfulness is perhaps as much a part of refusing to accept our limits, our mortality, as of anything else. Youth is exceptionally arrogant in its self-belief. Have you ever met an eighteen-year-old male who did not think, at least in practice, that he was going to live forever? I certainly believed as much at that age. And now, in my late thirties, I do my level best to recapture that feeling—keeping my weight down, running and cycling as much as I can, avidly examining race results to see how many teenagers and twentysomethings I managed to burn off in the last half a mile. Of course, keeping fit is somewhat Janus-faced in this regard: you stay healthy, but the law of diminishing returns with regard to training and results also makes you acutely aware that time is, slowly but surely, closing in on you.

Of course, you don't have to be a keep-fit fanatic to engage in the cult of youth. If you cannot be bothered with all that exercise palaver—"a bit too much like hard work"—there are other ways of conning yourself into thinking that you are going to cheat the Grim Reaper. For example, I can always tell when I'm waiting at the airport in a line which contains a high proportion of Americans. Such lines usually contain an abnormally high proportion of older men sporting dreadful toupees, dye-jobs, and obvious hair-transplants. Not that Americans are peculiarly depraved when it comes to bad strategies with regard to hair; I suspect they simply have more money to indulge in such disasters and live in a culture where people are too afraid to state the obvious. Why, I ask myself, would someone who weighs 300 pounds and is obviously the wrong side of 60 bother wearing such a dreadful orange toupee? But there you go; it happens all too frequently; and the rest of us must learn to deal with it.

Yet there is an even more sinister side to the cult of youth than even the wearing of orange toupees. For all that youth and youthfulness are great marketing opportunities in contemporary Western society, for all that they represent a desire to avoid facing the reality of the progression of time and the inevitability of our own mortality, they are also inextricably linked with an obvious childishness or infantilism in society in general. As youth has become something which is aesthetically desirable, so the immature values of youth have become increasingly acceptable within adult society as a whole. Just look at the behavior of the celebrities who play such a profound role in the world in which we live, combining lives of massive overindulgence and childishness (remember how Mariah Carey doesn't "do" stairs? What about Michael Jackson's Neverland Ranch? Or Tom Cruise's prancing around on the chat show sofa?) with ridiculously portentous pronouncements on all manner of adult issues, from abortion to world poverty, about which they really know next to nothing? These are people who have never developed beyond the teenage years; but, while most of us had to make do as teenagers with stealing traffic cones to wear at silly parties, snarling at our parents, and pontificating over a pint or two about how we could change the world, these people have whole TV programs worshipfully devoted to them. The values of the ridiculous and pampered teenage years transformed into the value-system of an entire self-absorbed culture. As youth sells, so, as a result, does immaturity. Hopefully, most of us grew out of teenage silliness; it was fun, but it was right that it came to an end. What is so worrying is that the marketing of youth seems to go hand in hand with the promotion of childishness as a way of life; and the societies which are most advanced in terms of their consumer economies are so often the societies where childishness in adult, public life is so prized. Whether it is the infantile black and white rhetoric of politicians speaking on complex and subtle issues, the trivializing immaturity of so much postmodern thought, or the constant need for entertainment even in classrooms and church, reversion to childishness seems the order of the day in the West.

Consumerism is often criticized for the way in which it exalts individual choice at the expense of all else, with the result that value becomes simply a function of the marketplace. Yet I would argue that it is not only the fact that consumerism has led to an exaltation of choices in themselves which makes it responsible for the reductionist notion of value; it is the fact that consumerism has actually made the wrong choice. In its identification of youth as **the** significant market product, it has backed immaturity over age, foolishness over wisdom, know-it-all arrogance over humble acknowledgment of limitations and mortality. And those societies—be they economic states or even local churches—which choose to build themselves on consumerism need to realize sooner rather than later that the easy credit and self-centeredness which lie at the heart of their philosophical project can only manifest themselves in childishness. Childish rhetoric, childish ambitions, childish achievements.

Anti-ageing products are not only risky gifts to buy for your wife; perhaps they are even more dangerous than that. Perhaps they also symbolize a society determined to reverse the ageing—or should that be maturing?—process.

2.15

ZEN-CALVINISM AND THE ART
OF MOTORVEHICLE REPLACEMENT

Returning home late one night in the early summer, I found that my van's transmission had died. Fortunately, it happened on my driveway; unfortunately I needed to be at the airport at 6 am the following morning, which meant that I was placed almost permanently in the debt of the colleague who kindly crawled out of bed at 5 am and drove me the 35 miles to Philadelphia International. Still, it's an ill wind that blows no one any good, and it gave me the opportunity to replace the soccer-mom minivan with a slightly cooler, though just as antiquated, Dodge Neon. Given my compulsive need for almost constant rock music, it is also useful to have a four-CD capacity in the audio system.

While doing the paperwork at the dealership for the "new" car, the salesman, noticing my accent, asked me what had brought me to the US. Teaching at a seminary, I responded. Well, well, he said, what a coincidence—the company for which he worked and from whom I was buying the car was a Christian company, owned by a Christian, and reflecting Christian values. At this point, I almost walked out—a Christian company? Give me an honest Jew, Muslim, agnostic, atheist, tree-hugger, or Memphis-based Presleyterian worshiper of "the King," but, when it comes to service and integrity in business, keep me away from Christians!

Why do I say this? Well, when I cast my eye over the 22 years of my time as a Christian, I realize I've just about seen it all done by those who name the name of Christ: homosexuality, adultery, stalking, theft, lies, sexual abuse of minors, threats, fraud, wife-beating, defamation, bullying, backbiting, greediness, heresy, and general all-round loutishness. And as for the language of grace and forgiveness—well, as American talk show guests might say, "Don't even go there!" Frankly, I have lost count of the times that such language has been used to excuse and then baptize and sanctify substandard behavior, moral and professional. The bottom line: in my experience, Christians can be horrible people; and, basically, they cannot be trusted to sell you chewing gum, let alone a used car.

It's disappointing, given that Christianity claims to hold the key to the meaning of life, the universe, and everything. Even more disappointing, one might add, when the church also claims to represent the claims of a righteous and holy God on earth, and to foreshadow the great heavenly community which will be brought into full and final existence at the end of time. Given all this, I should surely have stood up and walked out of the car dealership and taken my business elsewhere.

But I didn't; and the reasons I didn't was simply these—first, my wife is Scottish and knows a good (i.e. cheap) car when she sees one; and, second, I am a committed Zen-Calvinist, and thus able to face life as it really is without being particularly disturbed by it. Indeed, it is only my Zen-Calvinism which keeps me sane (though some might dispute the appropriateness of applying that word to myself).

So what is Zen-Calvinism? Like the Buddhist movement which shares the same name, Zen-Calvinism is a school of religious thought which allows its adherents to live at one with the world, untroubled in any ultimate sense by the slings and arrows which life throws their way. It is also counter-cultural and thus represents a deeply alternative lifestyle. Let me elaborate a little on this countercultural mentality.

At the heart of Zen-Calvinism is the belief that all human beings are morally flawed, unlike the world-views projected by the celebrity-saturated commercial culture of the modern West. In the latter, imperfection is conceived of as a lack of happiness, in turn understood as lack of access to products, broadly conceived, be they fast cars, fame, beauty, or power. At root, we could say that, in the West, human imperfection comes increasingly to be seen as a lack of money—because money can buy any or all of these things and thus enable us to become perfect. In fact, of course, this culture is itself profoundly flawed and ultimately self-defeating—money, like crack cocaine, gives short-term fixes but the experience of buying something lasts only a moment. And, for the record, I believe this is because it is not the buying of *products* which ultimately drives consumerism; it is the *buying* of products which does this (that's one for a future Wages piece). When I buy something, then for a split second, I become god; I, Carl Trueman, use my divine powers to transubstantiate a worthless piece of paper or plastic into a loaf of bread, a book, a car, a house. This momentary self-deification satisfies my idolatry of self, but only for a moment; it has to be repeated again and again and again if I am to keep myself persuaded that I am indeed god, master of all I survey.

In contrast to this, Zen-Calvinism understands that the human predicament is not solved by such rampant consumption; in fact, this consumption is itself a manifestation of the human desire to throw off responsibility to God and deify humanity itself. It also acknowledges the futile nature of this consumption, that the fleeting kicks and thrills it gives are in the end just so many reminders of our own mortality. In its place, it acknowledges its morally flawed nature, its constant tendency to placing itself at the center of the universe, and puts dependence upon God, not consumptive flight from God, up front and central. Zen-Calvinists also accept that they are themselves no better than anyone else; and, understanding their own tendencies to treat everyone else in a less-than-perfect fashion, they will not be surprised when they are repaid in kind. Zen-Calvinists are at one with the depravity of the fallen universe; they expect to be treated as they know they have treated others.

The second major element of Zen-Calvinism are the mantras which we use to worship. Unlike those used to hide from reality, whether the latest Britney Spears ditty or some nostalgic song extolling the mythical virtues of yesteryear, the Zen-Calvinist mantra book is rooted in the 150 songs we find in the Bible's book of Psalms. Here, both Zen-Calvinist master and novice find words to express their deepest longings, their profoundest fears, and their most passionate desires in words which, as inspired by God, have the divine imprimatur. Indeed, there are words here that, if God had not declared "I have written these and they belong to me," we might hesitate to use them in an address to him. Yet here is a book which allows all human emotions to be expressed in the worship of God. Public and private spirituality built upon these words will, by definition, be both countercultural and equip us for life as it really is. Countercultural because we learn here that it is OK to be depressed, to be angry, to be frustrated, to be brokenhearted, and that the answer to these things is neither to pretend that they do not exist nor to "consume" our way out of them by pretending to be god ourselves and using our credit cards to flee from the Creator. The answer is rather to understand our fallen, finite, tragic condition, to face up to this in all its naked, stark reality, and then to look to the God of all history as the only ultimate source of stability in the present and happiness in the future.

The final element of Zen-Calvinism is perhaps the most important: the realization that all evil has been subverted for the greater good purposes of the God who loves his church. If the supreme crime of human history—the judicial murder of the very Son of God—can be used for the greatest good, then any other crime, sin, or moral failing can also be frustrated and turned to good account. And that applies not just to the loutish and corrupt behavior of others; it applies supremely to that of the Zen-Calvinist who reflects upon these things.

So that's why, against my better judgment, I didn't flee from the Christian car sales company, and how my Zen-Calvinism enabled me to buy the car with confidence. Yes, I expect to be ripped off and treated shabbily, especially by Christians, because I know they are no better than I am. Thankfully, at the time of writing, the particular car I bought has proved excellent value for money. This is clearly one Christian company that does take integrity seriously. But even if this was not the case, I would still have the weapons of the great Zen-Calvinist masters at my disposal to make sure that, far from driving me to despair, such behavior merely confirms what I already know about the universe (that it is fallen, just like me); it drives me again to my mantras (the inspired Psalms) which teach me to articulate reality and personal identity as it really is, not as some commercial tells me; and it points me to the ultimate reality (Jesus Christ, crucified and risen). Thus, if you want a real alternative lifestyle, get hold of Zen-Calvinism and turn on to the Psalms, tune in to the reality of depravity, and, with regards to consumerist idolatry, drop out.

Postscript

Sherlock Holmes and the Curious Case of the Missing Book

It was in the winter of '04 that I arrived at 221b Baker Street to find Holmes standing at the window, gazing over a snow covered London and chewing on the stem of his trusty pipe. Clearly exhausted by the demands of the events surrounding the grisly case of the Psychic Cat of Kuala Lumpur (a tale for which the world is not yet ready), he seemed preoccupied.

After a few minutes of silence, he declared, somewhat rhetorically (or so it seemed) "It is indeed a curious thing."

"What is that, Holmes?" I replied.

Holmes spun round and looked me in the eye. "Why, the missing book, Watson! The missing book! Like the dog that did not bark, so often in these cases it is that which should be there, but which so emphatically is not, that provides the most important details."

The missing book? I had, as usual kept a careful eye on the newspapers. The society pages had been full of the normal gossip and trivia; and there had been the typical round of petty crimes; but I had seen no reference anywhere to a missing book. Perhaps, I thought, some wealthy private book collector had been relieved of a volume of exceptional rarity; or maybe some society figure had found that a diary or journal of particular sensitivity had gone missing. "Has there been a theft?" I asked.

"In a manner of speaking. It is a curious thing, my friend, when a book which has enjoyed authority and common currency for so long should so dramatically have disappeared from the public arena."

"Come, come Holmes," I said, somewhat exasperated that my friend, while apparently addressing me, seemed rather to be speaking to himself. "Tell me, of what book are you speaking?"

Holmes drew deeply on his pipe and then blew a perfect smoke ring into the air. "Why, The Gospel of John, my dear old friend. It is surely a strange and somewhat disturbing thing that a book which the church recognized so early in its history as being an authoritative part of the biblical canon has over recent years all but disappeared from some of the most influential Christological writings, even in apparently evangelical quarters."

"Why, Holmes, that's preposterous!" I declared. "So many crucial theological doctrines are stated in the Gospel of John that, if this book has truly gone missing, the world of Christian belief stands in serious jeopardy."

"Ahh, Watson. I can always rely on the blunt common sense of the British medical man to see the obvious things which those of more subtle minds can tend to miss. You are, of course, absolutely correct. The doctrine of the Trinity—that doctrine which defines the very particular identity of the Christian God over against all impostors—becomes incalculably more difficult to defend once John has gone missing. Then there are the other cardinal points of orthodoxy—the messianic self-consciousness of Jesus, the christological hope of Israel in the Old Testament... The construction of Christologies based on only the Synoptic Gospels will be highly deviant in a number of ways that are potentially lethal to the gospel. Souls will die, Watson, mark my words. Souls will surely die."

"But who would do such a thing?" I asked, the full terror of Holmes's words dawning on me. "Who would steal the Gospel of John when the testimony of history is so much in the book's favour, and the implications of such a theft for the Good News are so devastating?"

"I suspect my old rival, Professor Moriarty. For years now he has been laying the ground work for this theft, arguing that John's worldview was too heavily influenced by Greek thought and by ontological categories. He claims that it thus represents a layer of philosophical paganism which distorts the simple message of the gospel." Holmes put down his pipe and strolled over to his violin case. His hands stroked the black lacquer case. He removed the Stradivarius and began to play.

At length, I responded. "That's true, but he was arrested and sentenced to life imprisonment for that. If I remember, the judge declared that his arguments were among the most criminally specious he had ever heard."

"True, Watson, true. But, as you know, Moriarty is such an outwardly pleasant, urbane and learned man that the governor of his prison allowed him to leave after serving only part of his sentence. Thus, last Tuesday, he was once again, I am told, a free man. Within hours of his release, the Gospel of John had started mysterously to disappear even from some well-known evangelical theologies. Inspector Lestrade has rounded up the usual suspects and started interviewing them. Some of them are talking already. It would appear that a variety of reasons has been given for the disappearances. Some have trotted out the hackneyed Hellenism argument; others have argued that to construct a purely Synoptic Christology is no more or less controversial than to construct one using all four gospels; a number have argued that John is self-evidently not 'history' in the way that Matthew, Mark, and Luke are; then there are a few who argue that theology is really narrative, and that the kind of ontological questions introduced by the Gospel of John are not consistent with the basic thrust of redemptive history."

"My, my, Holmes. This is disturbing. What can be done to counter such arguments before it's too late?"

"Several lines of refutation suggest themselves." Holmes replaced the violin in its case and gazed out of the window.

"The Hellenism argument is the most tedious," he sighed. "It has been dealt with so many times over the years that I find I have no interest in mounting a refutation."

"But what about those who say that to build a Christology on four gospels is just as controversial a theological move as to build one on three? This would seem a reasonable point to make, Holmes, would it not?"

Holmes chuckled. "Superficially plausible but utterly wrongheaded. As usual, my dear fellow, you see the alleged scholarly rationale but you do not observe the theological pre-suppositions. When the church has recognised four gospels as authoritative since at least the time of Irenaeus in the second century, it is those who opt for the three rather than the four who make the contentious and highly theological and philosophical move. For anyone who takes biblical authority seriously, four is the biblical default; three requires extra-biblical philosophical justification."

He continued: "Of course, on one level, it is clear—indeed, somewhat obvious even to most children in Sunday School—that each of the gospels tells the story of Jesus from a different perspective, placing the emphasis in different places. There is nothing wrong, therefore, with producing books which deal with, say, the Christology of the synoptics, or of John or of Matthew, etc. As long as the writer keeps in mind that each gospel is ultimately not teaching anything which is inconsistent with any other of the gospels, and all conclusions are checked for consistency with the teaching of the whole of canonical scripture, then such studies can be most helpful in bringing out the riches and variety of emphases in the Bible. The problem is, of course, that even evangelical scholars have increasingly judged John's teaching as having little or no significance for the synoptics. This has then allowed them to construct arguments which deny things clearly taught in John, such as pre-existence and messianic self-consciousness."

Holmes had a reputation for being notoriously arrogant, and his next comment indicated why; "The only surprise to me is that so many evangelical scholars seem so ignorant of history that they can seriously make this case about Hellenism and about privileging the synoptics over John, as if it were some kind of original insight and not a hackneyed old heresy. Still, isn't that always the case? Yesterday's tired old liberalism is today's cutting-edge evangelicalism."

"Holmes," I protested "You can be insufferably arrogant at times!"

"Just because I am insufferably arrogant does not make my comments on biblical scholarship necessarily untrue, my dear chap. As to this business of John not being history in the manner of, say, Matthew, Mark, and Luke, this argument too is not of particularly recent vintage. It is built rather upon Enlightenment notions of what does and does not constitute historical writing. The whole thesis is thus somewhat modernist, and should be equally implausible both to orthodox evangelicals and postmodern historians. At least, it should be so in theory. Strange to tell, the selective attitude to the Enlightenment exhibited by many evangelicals and postmodern pundits means that the Gospel of John has continued to suffer from the suspicion of not teaching the truth in any manner, straightforward or otherwise. This has left it very vulnerable to being stolen."

"True enough, Holmes. But what about the argument that a Christology built upon the synoptic gospels is more true to the basic narrative structure of truth as exhibited in the redemptive historical structure of the Bible?"

Holmes picked up his pipe once more. "As to the notion of *narrative*, when this is introduced as being the overarching device for expressing truth, or as guiding all Bible teaching, then an alien philosophical framework is being introduced as an apriori principle for reading scripture. Certainly, there is much narrative in scripture, but to use this as the only axiomatic model for understanding and explicating the gospel is fallacious. First, this approach ignores the fact that much of the Bible is not narratival in structure.

"Second, this kind of approach fails to historicise itself by understanding that the use of narrative in this way arises in the context of modern, anti-metaphysical, anti-ontological philosophy. It is potentially just as enslaved to

219

unbiblical philosophical paradigms as any of the early Greek Apologists.

"Third, to make a radically narratival redemptive historical approach to scripture into an all-embracing, methodologically exclusive ideology is an absurd act of shortsighted, unbiblical, anti-historical intellectual hubris. It confuses an insight, a tool, with the whole toolkit. Doing theology by using nothing more than redemptive history is like trying to build a house from the ground up, armed only with a hammer. Futile, old chap, utterly futile.

"Fourth, it fails to realize that narratives themselves only have coherence transcendence when co-ordinated with the kind of transcendent ontology and metaphysics taught in the Gospel of John."

At this, I could contain myself no longer. "But if we lose ontology and metaphysics, Holmes, then, if you are right, surely we will also lose universality?" I exclaimed.

"How true, Watson. Each community ends up with its own narrative. The Baptist, the Anglican, the Presbyterian, the Mennonite, the Catholic, even the White Supremacist— all have their own community narratives, and none can be critiqued from the outside. Even immanent critique based upon internal inconsistency becomes virtually impossible. If you relegate or reject all evidence in the canon which might militate against your pet theories, of course, you can get away with saying anything."

"The implications are terrifying, Holmes." My mind was racing, filled with thoughts of all that the church now stood to lose.

"Indeed, indeed. The pre-existence of the Son; the messianic self-consciousness of Jesus; the hope of Israel; the Trinitarian nature of God; even, as I have implied, the universal call, demand and promise of the gospel are rendered highly questionable. All are disappearing even from the pages of evangelical biblical theologies. And while the Gospel of John remains missing, we have little material with which to fight back."

Holmes' eyes blazed and he spoke with an urgency I have only heard on a handful of occasions. "The game's afoot,

Watson. The gospel is in jeopardy and the most frightening aspect of this whole case is that it is in danger from the very people who have been charged to protect, defend and proclaim it. If we cannot persuade the next generation of evangelical thinkers that the missing gospel must be found, then it is all over for Christianity as we know it. This, my dear fellow, is a four pipe problem." With that, Holmes returned to gazing of the window and I knew it was time for him to think and for me to leave. I pulled on my coat, went back out into the snow. The wind seemed even colder than it had when I arrived. I hailed a hansom cab and headed back to my rooms, with Holmes' words echoing in my mind: "Souls will die, Watson, mark my words. Souls will surely die."

Christian Focus Publications

publishes books for all ages

Our mission statement –

STAYING FAITHFUL

In dependence upon God we seek to help make His infallible Word, the Bible, relevant. Our aim is to ensure that the Lord Jesus Christ is presented as the only hope to obtain forgiveness of sin, live a useful life and look forward to heaven with Him.

REACHING OUT

Christ's last command requires us to reach out to our world with His gospel. We seek to help fulfill that by publishing books that point people towards Jesus and help them develop a Christ-like maturity. We aim to equip all levels of readers for life, work, ministry and mission.

Books in our adult range are published in three imprints.

Christian Focus contains popular works including biographies, commentaries, basic doctrine and Christian living. Our children's books are also published in this imprint.

Mentor focuses on books written at a level suitable for Bible College and seminary students, pastors, and other serious readers. The imprint includes commentaries, doctrinal studies, examination of current issues and church history.

Christian Heritage contains classic writings from the past.

Christian Focus Publications, Ltd
Geanies House, Fearn, Ross-shire,
IV20 1TW, Scotland, United Kingdom
info@christianfocus.com

www.christianfocus.com